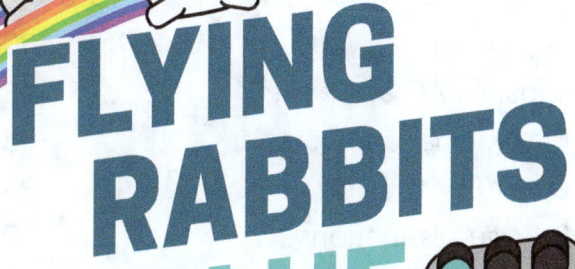

FLYING RABBITS and BLUE TRAFFIC LIGHTS

(JAPANESE YOU DIDN'T KNOW YOU WANTED TO KNOW)

気になる日本語

デビット・ベネット
DAVID BENNETT

CONTENTS

Introduction 2
Say What?? 20
Japanese That Counts 48
Made In Japan—Sort Of 68
Don't Be So Contradictory 88
Precise Distinctions 108
Kanji Panic 2: Revenge Of Kanji 132
Explain This To Me 160
Writing Right 184
David's Diction Academy 210

Table of Hiragana 236
Table of Katakana 237
Full List of Entries 238
項目一覧 242
Index 246

積んじゃだめ!
TOO GOOD TO PILE UP!

What's the meaning and origin of the expression 積読 *tsundoku*?

積読 *tsundoku* is the act of leaving a book unread after buying it, typically piled up with other unread books.

It's a compound of 積む *tsumu* ('to pile up') and 読 *doku* ('to read', 'reading').

But it's also a pun on 積んどく *tsundoku*, which is a contraction of 積んで *tsunde* + おく *oku* ('to pile something up' + 'to leave untouched').

Anyway, you won't need to worry about that happening with . . .

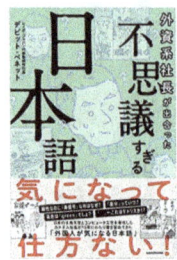

日本語版も読みたいですか？

可愛い漫画やショートイッセーも入ってます！

Published in Japanese in print and ebook format by KADOKAWA. Search for 978-4-04-604605-5 on Amazon.jp.

Flying Rabbits and Blue Traffic Lights
(Japanese You Didn't Know You Wanted to Know)
978-1-77342-101-8

David Bennett

Book development:
IndieBookLauncher.com

Editing and Review (Japanese):
Ikuko Komuro-Lee

Editing and Review (English):
Jotaro Arimori, Shane Bennett, Chris Butcher, Brian Chapman, Franz DeLeon, Jocelyn Iizuka, Tracy McDonald, Tommy Tomihara, Andrew Woodrow-Butcher

Typesetting, Design, and Illustration:
Saul Bottcher

Notice of Rights
All text and images copyright 2022 David Bennett, all rights reserved.

Also available
Ebook edition, ISBN 978-1-77342-107-0
Japanese edition, ISBN 978-4-04-604605-5
(published in Japan by KADOKAWA)

目次

はじめに......................3
何、これ?!..................... 21
日本語で数えよう!............. 49
日本製…かな?................. 69
それ、矛盾してない?!.......... 89
厳密に言えば.................. 109
漢字パニック2:ザ・リベンジ....... 133
頼む、教えてくれ!.............. 161
正しい書き方.................. 185
デビットの日本語アカデミー....... 211

ひらがな50音表................ 236
カタカナ50音表................ 237
Full List of Entries................ 238
項目一覧..................... 242
Index....................... 246

デビット・ベネット DAVID BENNETT

INTRODUCTION

Why I Wrote This Book 4
Meet Your Teachers 8
Using This Book 12
Pronouncing Japanese 13
Know Your ABC's—In Japanese 14

はじめに

はしがき．．．．．．．．．．．．．．．．．．．．．．．．．．．．．．．4
先生の紹介．．．．．．．．．．．．．．．．．．．．．．．．．．．．．8
本書の使い方．．．．．．．．．．．．．．．．．．．．．．．．12
発音の仕方．．．．．．．．．．．．．．．．．．．．．．．．．．13
日本語の表記法．．．．．．．．．．．．．．．．．．．．．．14

デビット・ベネット DAVID BENNETT

はしがき
WHY I WROTE THIS BOOK

I began studying Japanese in 1994, my first year of high school, and I quickly realized that I was terrible at learning languages. I struggled with many concepts:

- Why do you count by units of 10,000? How will I ever be able to communicate numbers on the fly?
- Why do you write it "ha", but say it "wa", and there's no direct English translation?
- There are four "alphabets", and you mix-and-match them depending on what you're writing about?

Many times over the course of my studies I would learn something and think to myself, "How does this make any sense at all?"

I inundated my teachers and professors with questions. "If this means this, then why doesn't that mean that?!" . . . it was endless.

In 2004, I was accepted to the Japan Exchange and Teaching Programme (JET)

and was on my way to live in Japan for the second time. It was then that I joined a website called *Big Daikon,* which, at the time, was an essential source of information on the JET program and living in Japan.

One of the discussion threads on *Big Daikon* invited advanced speakers to share difficult Japanese they had learned and to answer questions from their peers. People started to share interesting or perplexing words, phrases and grammar that they had discovered during their studies.

When I brought some of these tidbits to my native Japanese-speaking friends, their responses ranged from "I never knew that!" to "Why is that interesting?" and "Now I get it. That makes sense!"

I began assembling a collection of curious facts about the Japanese language. I wrote down the first few entries, then I created a file on my computer as the number grew. That file has remained open ever since.

WHY I WROTE THIS BOOK • あとがき

Since beginning my journey, I've had many teachers and attended Japanese language classes with students from around the world. After the JET program I went on to help teach an introductory Japanese language course at the University of Toronto in Canada, and to study at Waseda University in Japan.

I found that living in Japan gave me insights into my own country. Similarly, when it comes to the Japanese language, I believe there's a lot to learn from a non-native speaker's questions.

This book is the culmination of those years spent collecting, categorizing, and researching interesting Japanese words, phrases and peculiarities. I believe language lovers, students of Japanese, and native Japanese speakers will all find the topics covered in this book fascinating.

A special thank you to everyone that has helped me on this journey and spent countless hours editing, correcting, and giving me ideas for the book. My brilliant editor and childhood friend, Saul Bottcher. My brother Shane Bennett and sister Tracy McDonald, and my dear friends Chris Butcher, Andrew Woodrow-Butcher, Franz DeLeon, Jotaro Arimori, Tommy Tomihara, Jocelyn Iizuka, and my first friend at Waseda University, Brian Chapman.

An extra special thank you to Ikuko Komuro-Lee, Associate Professor of Japanese Language at the University of Toronto for bearing the brunt of most of my questions, and for giving me the tools and the confidence to learn Japanese.

Finally, a thank you to my family. My wife Kiko, my eldest son Noa, my daughter Hana, and my youngest son Kei. They are the reason I do anything and everything.

—David Bennett, Tokyo, 2022

先生の紹介
MEET YOUR TEACHERS

Welcome to my classroom! I'll be leading the lesson, but I have a few helpers you may like to meet:

FROG • カエル *kaeru*

> "Japanese is fun! I'll be helping you with examples and useful tips along the way."

Frog hopped in the window one day. He was so cheerful, we decided to keep him around.

Occupation: Student.

Likes: Pocky, J-Pop, and trips to the beach.

BLOSSOM • さくら *sakura*

> "I'll teach you about Japanese etiquette and social customs. I might tell you the occasional folk tale, too."

Blossom lives on my desk. She's pretty calm and likes to observe and learn.

Occupation: Diplomat.

Likes: Dressing up in kimono, eating sushi, and reading *Nansou Satomi Hakkenden*.

MEET YOUR TEACHERS • 先生紹介

BENTO • 弁当 *bentou*

> When you're ready to *really* appreciate Japanese, you'll be happy you came to me.

Somebody left him behind after lunch last year. He's only gotten crustier since then.

Occupation: Nobody's sure, but he takes it very seriously.

Likes: Navy blue sweaters, history books, and doing things correctly.

KUIZU • クイズ *kuizu*

これでいいのだ！

We're not actually sure where Kuizu hides. He just pops up whenever—

It's quiz time!!

. . . not now, Kuizu. Wait a few more pages. Where were we?

Occupation: Quiz host.

Likes: Pretty much anything, as long as it's in quiz form.

You bet!!

デビット・ベネット DAVID BENNETT

本書の使い方
USING THIS BOOK

This book is written in a question-and-answer format. You can read the questions in any order you like.

For each question, you'll get a straight answer from me (David), followed by any helpful comments my assistants want to add. (They tend to be quite talkative.)

If you ever want to look up a specific word or phrase, or you want a list of all entries, just refer to the indexes starting on page 238.

Whenever you see Japanese words in the book, they'll look like this:

皮肉 *hiniku* ('sarcasm' or 'irony')

The first part is the Japanese written form, followed by the pronunciation, and the last part (in brackets) is the meaning.

発音の仕方
PRONOUNCING JAPANESE

Japanese pronunciation is very consistent. There are five vowels, and they always sound like this:

> **a** jar   **o** toe
> **e** set   **u** blue
> **i** bee

Double vowels (*aa ee ii oo uu*) sound the same, but you hold the sound for longer. The combination *ou* sounds the same as *oo*. An elongated vowel can change the meaning of a word, so speak carefully!

The consonants all sound fairly close to their English counterparts, except for **r**, which sounds about halfway between English "r" and English "l".

Easy, right? If you're a beginner, there's just one more thing you should know before you dive into the book . . .

デビット・ベネット DAVID BENNETT

日本語の表記法
KNOW YOUR ABC'S—IN JAPANESE

What's up with Japanese writing? Some of it looks like Chinese characters, other parts look rounder and more simple, and I even see English letters and numbers here and there.

Japanese uses several writing systems for different purposes.

In English, it's simple: we use the Roman alphabet, which has twenty-six letters, each with capital and lower-case forms. For numbers, we use the ten Arabic numerals, 0 to 9.

> If you want to be precise (and you do), we actually use two systems of writing in English: printed and *cursive* . . .

> However, since these two styles are entirely interchangeable, most people think of English as having a single writing system.

In Japanese, things are a little more complicated. There are several writing systems that are each used for a specific purpose. The first two are for directly representing the spoken sounds:

りんご　くるま　おもちゃ

Hiragana is a set of 46 characters that represent the sounds of the Japanese language. It's used for native Japanese words.

KNOW YOUR ABC'S—IN JAPANESE • 日本語の表記法

デビット　ソール　パン

Katakana is another set of 46 characters, representing the same sounds as hiragana. It's used for foreign words that have been brought into the Japanese language.

Hiragana and katakana were both created from simplifications of Chinese characters hundreds of years ago. For example:

阿→あ　　　　　以→い

礼→レ　　　　　止→ト

Katakana characters are sharper and more angular than hiragana characters.

> This visual difference might remind you of printed and cursive letters in English, but remember, hiragana and katakana each have a specific purpose. They aren't interchangeable.

The next writing system is a bit different.

緑　　青　　白

<u>Kanji</u> are characters borrowed from written Chinese. They're a compact way to represent words, sounds, or ideas. They're spoken using the same set of sounds as hiragana and katakana, but most kanji characters can be read more than one way, with a different meaning for each reading. A typical adult needs to

>>>

KNOW YOUR ABC'S—IN JAPANESE • 日本語の表記法

know about 2000 kanji characters to be literate in Japanese.

> That might sound like a lot, but keep in mind that native English speakers often know 20,000 words or more.

These three writing systems cover the majority of Japanese text, but there are two more used for special purposes:

The Roman alphabet is used for foreign acronyms, such as "DVD". It's also used at times to make words of phrases seem more foreign or unique. For example, some celebrities write their names using the Roman alphabet.

Arabic numerals are used for numbers, just like in English!

When you read Japanese text, you'll find that hiragana, katakana, and kanji characters are often used in the same sentence. In this example, you can see all five writing systems used together in a common and simple sentence:

東京タワーの1階でDVDを売っています
Toukyou tawaa no ikkai de DVD wo utteimasu.
"They sell DVDs on the 1st floor of Tokyo Tower."

Here are the kanji characters:
東京タワーの1階でDVDを売っています

Here's the hiragana:
東京タワーの1階でDVDを売っています

And here's the katakana:
東京タワーの1階でDVDを売っています

Finally, Arabic numerals and Roman letters:
東京タワーの1階でDVDを売っています

. . . and now, on to the book!

デビット・ベネット DAVID BENNETT

SAY WHAT??

For all those strange sayings that leave you scratching your head . . .

Stretched Octopus?? 22
Holy Mackerel! I've Been Robbed! . . . 24
Spittin' Samurai 26
You Need To Go The Whole 19.64km 30
Meaty Sarcasm. 32
Bye, I'm Home! 36
A Humble Greeting 38
Proverbial Japanese 41

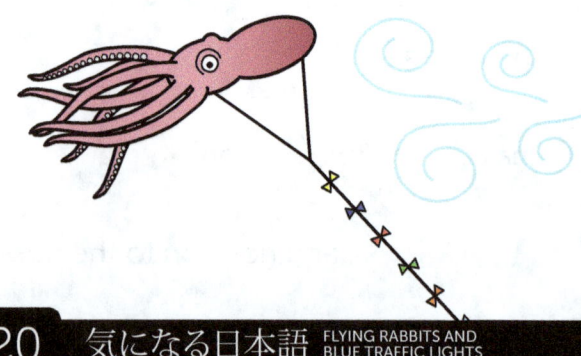

何、これ?!
みんなに「何これ?!」のお答えします

引っ張られてるタコ? 22
サバの泥棒 24
侍のカウボーイ 26
19.64キロまで 30
肉のある皮肉 32
さようなら、帰って来たよ! 36
丁寧な挨拶 38
ことわざ 41

デビット・ベネット DAVID BENNETT

引っ張られてるタコ?
STRETCHED OCTOPUS??

What does 引っ張りだこ *hipparidako* ('stretched octopus') mean?

引っ張りだこ *hipparidako* refers to someone or something that's very popular, or in high demand. It's something you might say when you're talking about a pop star.

> A comparable English phrase would be "selling like hotcakes".

> Oh . . . and it also means octopus meat stretched out to dry.

> You can eat dried octopus meat as a snack, or use it as an ingredient in a dish.

And what's the correct kanji character to use for たこ *tako* ('octopus') in *hipparidako*?

The original kanji character for the *tako* at the end of 引っ張りだこ *hipparidako* was 蛸 *tako* ('octopus').

> Lately though, 凧 *tako* ('kite'), or its hiragana form たこ *tako*, are being used more often, possibly because such flights of popularity tend to be short and can crash unexpectedly. •

サバの泥棒
HOLY MACKEREL! I'VE BEEN ROBBED!

What does the expression サバを読む *saba wo yomu* ('to count mackerels' or literally 'to read a mackerel') mean, and why?

It means to exaggerate, or to manipulate figures to your own advantage.

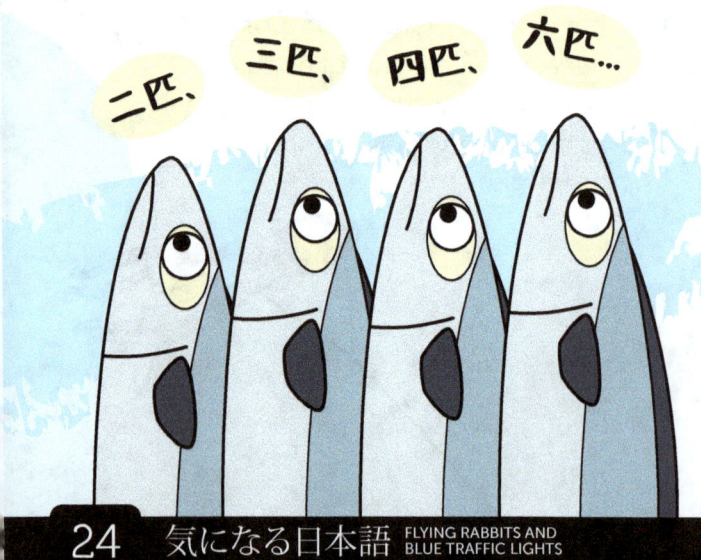

 Mackerels rot quickly, so in the past in Japan they were counted quickly—often to the advantage of the seller.

 This isn't an expression you'll hear out on the street, but it tends to pop up in books containing proverbs or old stories, and often baffles modern readers. •

侍のカウボーイ
SPITTIN' SAMURAI

What does the expression ヤニ下がる *yani sagaru* ('to spit nicotine') mean, and when is it used?

ヤニ下がる *yani sagaru* means 'to look smug' or 'to try to look cool' . . . so what does that have to do with nicotine?

> Traditionally, people in Japan used a long pipe called a 煙管 *kiseru* to smoke finely-shredded tobacco.

> A *kiseru* should never be pointed upward, or the bitter tobacco juices will run down into your mouth. If that happened, you'd need to ヤニ下がる *yani sagaru*—spit the juices out.

If you imagine someone trying to smoke a *kiseru* to look cool, but failing and needing to **yani sagaru**, you can see how the expression might have developed.

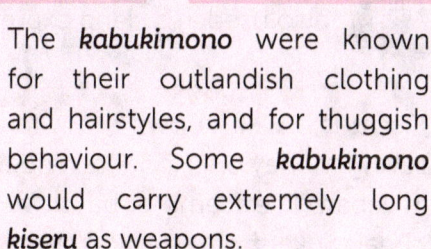

There's a historical angle to consider as well. In the Edo period (1603–1868), gangs of fallen samurai known as 傾奇者 *kabukimono* emerged.

The *kabukimono* were known for their outlandish clothing and hairstyles, and for thuggish behaviour. Some *kabukimono* would carry extremely long *kiseru* as weapons.

It's possible that using a *kiseru* to look cool may have originated as an attempt to imitate the *kabukimono*.

SPITTIN' SAMURAI • 侍のカウボーイ

Now for an example. Imagine a friend has bought a new car, but is acting smug. You might say:

「なにヤニさがってんの?!」
Nani yani sagatten no?!
What are you looking so pleased with yourself for?!

 Interestingly, the word *kiseru* is also used in a slang expression.

Kiseru is a well-known scam for saving money on a long train ride in Japan. The scammer buys two cheap tickets, one starting at the first stop, and the other ending at the final stop, but neither one covering the full journey . . .

What's the connection? A *kiseru* is typically made with a wooden shaft, a metal bowl, and a metal mouthpiece.

In the train ticket scam, *kiseru* refers to the fact that you give 'metal' (coin) for the two ends, but not for the middle.

If the *kabukimono* were around today, they probably wouldn't pay at all!

19.64キロまで
YOU NEED TO GO THE WHOLE 19.64KM

Why does ごり押し *gorioshi* (literally 'push 19.64km') mean 'to steamroll, push through all opposition' or 'to push on, regardless of others'?

The metaphor is obvious: if you're facing opposition or have no help, you have a lot of pushing to do—and 19.64km is a long distance to push something! But why 19.64km in particular?

> In pre-modern Japanese (before 1868), 里 *ri* was a unit of distance, and 五里 *gori* is simply '5 ri'. The *ri* was about 3.93km, so *gori* would be about 19.64km. (Incidentally, the *ri* is much longer than the Chinese *li* that inspired it centuries earlier.)

Here's an example of how to use this expression:

ちょっとしたごり押しの後
Chotto shita gorioshi no ato . . .
After a little arm-twisting . . .

You might also use it when pushing a friend to follow through with something, or when a politician tries to push through an agenda.

 There's a second theory that suggests ごり押し *gorioshi* comes from fishermen scraping the bottom of a river to catch *gori* ('sculpin'), which no doubt would have been hard work as well! •

肉のある皮肉
MEATY SARCASM

Why does 皮肉 *hiniku* mean 'sarcasm' or 'irony', when the two kanji characters it's formed from are 皮 *kawa* ('skin') and 肉 *niku* ('meat')?

The word 皮肉 *hiniku* originally comes from the longer Buddhist saying 「**皮肉骨髄**」 *hinikukotsuzui*, which means 'to understand the essence of something'.

We already have a clue to the first half: 皮肉 *hiniku* refers to 'skin' and 'meat', which are the parts closer to the surface. The second half, 骨髄 *kotsuzui*, refers to 'bones' and 'marrow'—the deeper parts. So in the Buddhist saying, if you understand the skin, meat, bones, and marrow of something, you understand its complete essence.

However, if you only take the first half of the phrase, 皮肉 *hiniku* ('skin' and 'meat'), this implies that you don't understand the deeper essence—only the shallower aspects.

> From this origin, as time passed, 皮肉 *hiniku* became a common criticism for a person who failed to perceive or understand deeper meanings.

After that, an interesting transition occurred: 皮肉 *hiniku* came to mean 'irony'.

It's possible that this happened because 皮肉 *hiniku* was being used in situations where the person ought to have understood something more deeply—but ironically, did not. In other words, being used

MEATY SARCASM・肉のある皮肉

in ironic situations may have caused the meaning of 皮肉 *hiniku* to change so that it literally meant 'irony'.

> We usually translate 皮肉 *hiniku* as either 'sarcasm' or 'irony', but in reality, the meaning of 皮肉 *hiniku* is not so easy to translate directly.

> For example, 皮肉な言葉 *hiniku na kotoba* is best translated as 'cynical remarks'. That doesn't have anything to do with irony or sarcasm. However, going back to the 'skin-deep' metaphor of the word's origin, you can see how it's related.

Here are two more examples of *hiniku* in everyday sentences:

皮肉なことに
Hiniku na koto ni
Ironically enough . . .

彼女は彼の皮肉がわかるだろうか
Kanojo wa kare no hiniku ga wakaru darou ka?
I wonder if she understands his sarcasm?

I wish Blossom were here right now with one of her factoids!

Really?

彼女は彼の皮肉がわかるだろうか?

さようなら、帰って来たよ!
BYE, I'M HOME!

What are the origins of the common expressions さようなら *sayounara* ('goodbye'), and ただいま *tadaima* ('I'm home')?

They're usually written in hiragana, but once I saw their kanji characters and it didn't make any sense!

ただいま *tadaima* ('I'm home') is simply a short version of ただ今帰りました *tada ima kaerimashita* ('I've just now come home').

さようなら *sayounara* ('goodbye') is more complicated. It originally comes from 然様なら *sayou nara*, which means 'if that's so'.

You might be wondering what that has to do with 'goodbye'!

Imagine a friend tells you they need to get going. If you replied by saying "if that's so", what you really mean is "well, if you must".

Interestingly, English 'goodbye' has a similar history. The original phrase was "God be with you", but over time it was contracted to "God b'wye". Then, in the late 1600's, 'God' changed to 'good', probably due to influence from "good morning" and "good evening".

By modern times, the spelling had settled to 'goodbye', and it became a ritualized phrase just like さようなら *sayounara*. •

丁寧な挨拶
A HUMBLE GREETING

Why do Japanese speakers say もしもし *moshimoshi* when answering the phone? This doesn't sound like any other Japanese word I know.

It evolved from a polite way of saying "I'm speaking", to check whether the phone was connected.

> *Moshimoshi* came into popularity when phones first began to be used in Japan. People would check whether the phone was connected by saying "I'm speaking . . . is anybody there?"

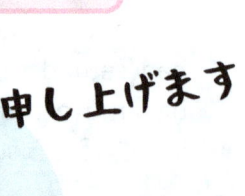

申し上げます

もしもし *moshimoshi* comes from 申し申し *moushimoushi*, which in turn was shortened from 申し上げます *moushiagemasu*, which is simply the humble form* of the verb 'to say'.

Interestingly, if someone came to your front door and opened it to inquire if anyone was at home, they'd use the same expression.

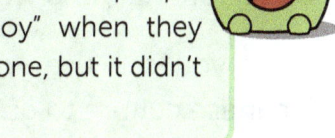

Fun fact: in English, Alexander Graham Bell wanted people to say "ahoy ahoy" when they answered the phone, but it didn't catch on. •

---

* You can learn more about humble language in *Mind Your Language* on page 212.

Contestants, get ready! How much do you know about Japanese proverbs?

In this quiz, you'll need to decide which sayings are real, and which are made-up!

See if you can use your knowledge of Japanese culture to guess correctly!

ことわざ
PROVERBIAL JAPANESE

1. When deciding whether to stand out or conform, remember that . . .

A 大きく鳴く鳥が先に食べる
Ookiku naku tori ga saki ni taberu.
The loudest bird gets fed first.

B 出る杭は打たれる
Deru kui wa utareru.
The nail that sticks out gets hammered down.

Parents often use this proverb to remind their children to remain well-behaved and agreeable.

Answer: B. *In Japanese culture, conformity is king. Sticking out or singing loudest will earn you scorn—not food.*

>>>

デビット・ベネット DAVID BENNETT

PROVERBIAL JAPANESE・ことわざ

2. If somebody is 猫を被る *neko wo kaburu* ("putting on the cat's face"), they're . . .

A Frowning because they had bad luck.

B Hiding their unpleasant personality behind an air of sweetness.

C Trying to appear cute to attract the attention of an important person.

D Putting on traditional Japanese stage makeup for a theatre performance.

>>>

Answer: B. Cats are associated with both good and bad luck in Japanese culture, but there is nothing that relates the cat's face to either kind of luck.

This expression first referred to **nekoda**, a type of matting or hat made from straw, used to cover yourself in the sun. This was later shortened to **neko**, and then replaced by **neko** ('cat'), though the meaning of covering or hiding one's self remains.

Cats are also notoriously hard to read, so perhaps the shift from **nekoda** to **neko** ('cat') was one that could happen easily.

PROVERBIAL JAPANESE・ことわざ

3. **If you're trying to decide whether to put total trust in an expert, remember that . . .**

A 猿も木から落ちる
Saru mo ki kara ochiru.
Even monkeys fall from trees.

B 琵琶のマスしか上流泳げない
Biwa no masu shika jouryuu oyogenai.
It takes a Biwa trout to swim upstream.

Answer: A. This proverb is famous in Japan. Monkeys climb trees all the time, so if even a monkey can fall out of a tree, then even an expert can be wrong. A similar proverb is かっぱの川流れ kappa no kawa nagare, "Even a kappa can be swept away in the river".

4. **If somebody is 馬の耳に念仏 uma no mimi ni nenbutsu ('whispering a Buddhist sutra in a horse's ear'), what they're doing is . . .**

A Elevating someone to a wealthier lifestyle.

B Wasting their effort.

Answer: B. Do you know any horses that like to contemplate philosophy? Probably not, so this would be a wasted effort.

Also, Buddhism teaches people to let go of material things, so a sutra shouldn't elevate anyone—horse or otherwise—to a wealthier lifestyle.

>>>

デビット・ベネット DAVID BENNETT

PROVERBIAL JAPANESE • ことわざ

5. When inviting guests to your home, remember the proverb that says . . .

A 女三人寄れば姦しい
Onna sannin yoreba kashimashii.
If three women gather, it's noisy.

B お邪魔するとお茶がでる
Ojama suru to ocha ga deru.
When visiting, one will (certainly) receive tea.

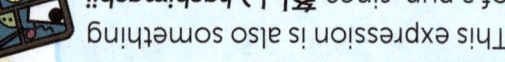

Answer: A. It's not a particularly modern sentiment, but this one is the real proverb.

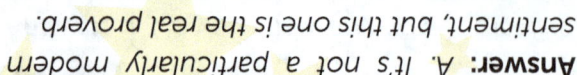

This expression is also something of a pun, since 姦しい *kashimashii* ("noisy, boisterous") is written with three small kanji characters for 'woman.'

6. If somebody's being 鬼に金棒 *oni ni kanabou* "an oni (ogre or demon) with an iron club", they're . . .

A Attacking a task more vigorously than necessary.

B Using a tool to do a job they couldn't manage without it.

Answer: A. Oni are fearsome creatures, often depicted with blue or red skin, wearing a loincloth, and carrying an iron club. If you call somebody "an oni with an iron club" it can have two meanings. The first is simply that they're invincible. The second meaning is that by carrying an iron club, the oni, which is already fearsome, has become even stronger—stronger than necessary.

デビット・ベネット DAVID BENNETT

JAPANESE THAT COUNTS

Wherein we learn that counting things in Japanese is much more complicated than one might expect.

Counting The Ways To Count 50
Become One With Broccoli 53
Flying Rabbits? 54
Counting Underpants 56
Not All Sushi Is Created Equal 58
Ballad Of The Ticket-Counter 60
Third Floor Two Ways? 62
Extreme Counting Showdown 65

日本語で数えよう！

日本語の数え方がややこしい！

数え方を数えよう！ 50
ブロッコリーの一つ… 53
飛べるウサギ？ 54
パンツを数える...................... 56
寿司は色々 58
意外と複雑 60
三階はなんで特別なの？............ 62
数えてみよう！ 65

デビット・ベネット DAVID BENNETT

数え方を数えよう!
COUNTING THE WAYS TO COUNT

Why are there so many ways to count in Japanese? Why can't I just use numbers like in English?

In English, counting is easy: five apples, five cars, five friends.

But in Japanese, you can almost never use the names of the numbers on their own for counting things.

> For example, if you want to count two of something, you can't just use the word 二 *ni* ('two'). That's because 二 *ni*, on its own, only refers to the *number* two.

Instead, when you want to count things in Japanese, you need to combine the number with a 'counter'.

A counter is a suffix that goes on the end of the number, to match it up with the thing you're counting.

You pick different counters depending on what you're counting. For example:

> 二匹の犬を飼ってます
> *Nihiki* **no inu wo kattemasu.**
> I have two dogs.

The counter 匹 *hiki* is used for counting small animals. Combining it with 二 *ni* lets you count the two dogs.

> English does have something similar. You buy two *loaves* of bread, or eat two *slices* of bread. But in English, certain of these words are optional, while in Japanese, they never are.

>>>

COUNTING THE WAYS TO COUNT • 数え方を数えよう！

> Thankfully, there are some general-purpose counters that you can use in a lot of situations.

Here are some examples:

一回しか行ってない

Ikkai shika ittenai.

I've only been once.

(回 *kai* counts occurences or events.)

二個しか食べてない

Niko shika tabetenai

I've only eaten two (of them).

(個 *ko* counts objects.)

> These are useful, but eventually, you'll need to master the more precise counters. And that's why we have this chapter! •

ブロッコリーの一つ…
BECOME ONE WITH BROCCOLI

What is the counter* for broccoli? Does the counter change if you break a stem off the main body?

When counting broccoli (ブロッコリー *burokkorii* in Japanese), you use 房 *fusa*, which translates as 'tuft', 'tassel', or 'bunch'.

> You'd count to three like this:
> 一房 *hitofusa*, 二房 *futafusa*, 三房 *mifusa*.

Fortunately, the counter for broccoli doesn't change if you break off a stem. •

---

* Counters are explained on page 50.

飛べるウサギ?
FLYING RABBITS?

Why is the character for 羽 *wa* ('wing') used as the counter* for rabbits, as opposed to the traditional counter for small animals, 匹 *hiki*?

Nobody knows the exact reason, but the most common explanation involves the dietary restrictions of Buddhist monks.

> In pre-modern Japan (before 1868), Buddhist monks weren't allowed to eat beef or other four-legged animal meat. However, chickens and other birds were exempted from this rule.

* Counters are explained on page 50.

Since rabbits could stand on two legs, and they happened to be plentiful, it's believed the monks classified the rabbits with the birds to allow the monks to eat rabbit meat.

It's definitely *not* because a rabbit's ears are long and floppy like a bird's wings!

Here's a peculiar fact for you: 飛び跳ねる *tobihaneru* is the word for jumping *and* for flying.

Of course, that's just a convenient coincidence . . . right? •

パンツを数える
COUNTING UNDERPANTS

What is the correct counter* for underpants?

The correct counter for underpants is 枚 *mai*, a counter for flat objects.

So why do I keep hearing people use 丁 *chou*?

This is a sort of joke or pun, and is also used mistakenly by children. A number of joking "explanations" have been invented to justify using 丁 *chou*.

> I don't see what's so funny about corrupting the Japanese language on purpose!

* Counters are explained on page 50.

The first "explanation" is that 丁 *chou* is also used for counting flat objects, and most people lay their underwear flat in the drawer.

Balderdash!

Others point out that 丁 looks like the 褌 *fundoshi* ('loincloth') worn by sumo wrestlers.

Ridiculous!!

But perhaps the best reason to use 丁 *chou* . . . is just to irritate people who are too picky.

Arrrggghhhhhh!!! •

寿司は色々
NOT ALL SUSHI IS CREATED EQUAL

What's the appropriate counter* for sushi?

It depends on the kind of sushi restaurant you're at!

At a conveyor belt sushi restaurant, you use 皿 *sara* ('dish', 'serving') to count the plates of sushi.

However, at a sit-down sushi restaurant, plates aren't used, so a different counter is needed.

> This is where it gets interesting! The counter varies depending on the type of sushi you're eating.

* Counters are explained on page 50.

貫 *kan* is for counting *nigirizushi* ('hand-pressed sushi'), which is the kind made with a bed of rice on the bottom and the fish (or other ingredient) on the top.

巻 *maki*, meanwhile, is used for *makizushi* ('rolled sushi'), which is the kind made by wrapping the rice and other ingredients in a long rectangular strip of seaweed, cucumber, or other material, then cutting the roll into small disc-shaped pieces.

Don't forget that your 山葵 *wasabi* goes on top of the sushi. Don't mix it in with your soy sauce!

Instead, hold the sushi (you can use your hands) and dip only the fish into the soy sauce, keeping the rice out. •

意外と複雑
BALLAD OF THE TICKET-COUNTER

Why does the counter* for a ticket change once you've used the ticket?

When you buy tickets (perhaps for a movie or concert), you count them as 一枚 *ichi mai*, 二枚 *ni mai*, and so on.

Here you're using 枚 *mai*, a counter for flat or thin objects.**

When you use a paper ticket, it would be torn in half. The counter then changes to 片 *hen* ('fragment' or 'imperfect'), a counter used for things that are worthless or have lost their value.

---

* Counters are explained on page 50.

** And also for underwear!

You would count your used tickets as 一片 *ippen*, 二片 *futahira*, 三片 *sanhira*, and so on. (Note: 片 can be read as either **hen** or **hira**.)

> For tickets that can win or lose, like a betting ticket at a horse race, or a lottery ticket, the initial tickets are still counted with 枚 *mai*.

> Losing tickets, which are now worthless, are counted with 片 *hen* instead.

> Meanwhile, winning tickets are counted with 本 *hon*, a counter for points or wins in sporting events. •

三階はなんで特別なの?
THIRD FLOOR TWO WAYS?

Why is 三階 *sankai* ('3rd floor') the only counter* for a floor of a building that can be read as either *kai* or *gai*?

There's no definitive answer, but it's probably because of a phenomenon seen in many languages: if there's an easier way to pronounce something, the easier way will eventually replace the hard way.

> In this case, it'd be an example of "voicing". A consonant that's beside a voiced sound will often become voiced itself. For example, in English, "rugs" is typically pronounced "rugz".

* Counters are explained on page 50.

Here are the phrases for the first ten floors of a building:

一階 *ikkai* ('1st floor')

二階 *nikai* ('2nd floor')

三階 *sankai* or *sangai* ('3rd floor')

四階 *yonkai* ('4th floor')

五階 *gokai* ('5th floor')

六階 *rokkai* ('6th floor')

七階 *nanakai* ('7th floor')

八階 *hachikai* or *hakkai* ('8th floor')

九階 *kyuukai* ('9th floor')

十階 *jukkai* or *jikkai* ('10th floor')

Don't forget, when you ask the question 何階 ("which floor?"), the 何階 can similarly be read as either *nankai* or *nangai*. •

IT'S QUIZ TIME!

Contestants, get ready! Think you know how to count in Japanese?

In this quiz we'll take a look at all the weird and wonderful counters you find in Japanese.

Can you sort out the real meanings from the fake ones? Remember, there might be more than one real meaning!

数えてみよう!
EXTREME COUNTING SHOWDOWN

1. If you're counting with 本 *hon*, what are you counting?

Choose one or several:

A long, cylindrical objects
B movies
C safe hits in baseball
D letters
E points in a karate match
F belts
G swords

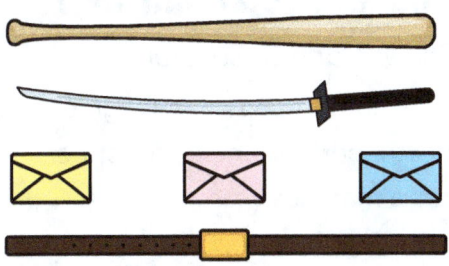

Answer: A, B, C, D, and E.

デビット・ベネット DAVID BENNETT

EXTREME COUNTING SHOWDOWN • 数えてみよう！

2. If you're counting with 口 *kou*, what are you counting?

Choose one or several:

- A chisels
- B teacups
- C praying mantises
- D slices of cake
- E swords
- F plant pots

Answer: A, B, D, E, and F.

3. If you're counting with 番 *ban*, what are you counting?

Choose one or several:

- A serial numbers
- B theatre performances
- C sumo matches
- D grapefruit
- E streets

Answer: A, B, C, D, and E.

4. If you're counting with 合 *gou*, what are you counting?

Choose one or several:

- A engagements in a fencing match
- B incense containers
- C mascot characters
- D ¹⁄₁₀ the height of a particular mountain

Answer: A, B, and D.

5. If you're counting with 丁 *chou*, what are you counting?

Choose one or several:

- A guns
- B oars
- C any long object
- D candles
- E cutlery
- F guitars

Answer: C is the correct answer.

MADE IN JAPAN—SORT OF

You might be surprised where some things were made . . . especially words!

DIY Kanji 70
ABC Sutra 72
Konnichi What? 76
From Russia With Salt 78
At the Viking Buffet 79
Lost In Translation 86

日本製…かな?

日本語みたい、でも実は日本語じゃない?!

自作漢字 70
ABCスートラ 72
こんにち何? 76
ロシアより塩を込めて 78
バイキングのバイキング 79
ロスト・イン・トランスレーション 86

デビット・ベネット DAVID BENNETT

自作漢字
DIY KANJI

Are there any kanji characters that were created in Japan, or were they all imported from China?

漢字 *kanji* literally translates to 'Chinese writing', and that's where almost all kanji characters came from. However, there are some kanji compounds that were invented in Japan. Most of them were invented in pre-modern times (before 1868), for existing native Japanese words.

> The expression 国字 *kokuji* ('national writing') refers to kanji characters created in Japan.

> Here's a list of some of the more commonly used kokuji:

hataraku	働く	to work
komu	込む	to be crowded
niou	匂う	to smell; be fragrant
hatake	畑	field of crops
sen	腺	gland
touge	峠	mountain pass
waku	枠	frame
hei	塀	fence
shiboru	搾る	to squeeze
sakaki	榊	*Cleyera japonica*
tsuji	辻	crossroads; street
shitsuke	躾	discipline; training; rearing

Cleyera japonica is a flowering evergreen, native to Japan and considered sacred in Shinto. •

ABCスートラ
ABC SUTRA

Do Japanese-speakers have an equivalent of the "ABC song" sung by English-speakers?

Yes, and its origins are fascinating!

There is a Japanese poem called the *Iroha*, which was first recorded in 1079 AD in ***Konkoumyousaishououkyou Ongi*** (*Readings of the Golden Light Sutra*).

The *Iroha* contains all the sounds of the Japanese language exactly once, which makes it a "perfect pangram".

> An *imperfect* pangram is one that contains all the sounds or letters of a language, but contains some of them *more than once*.

 "Pack my box with five dozen liquor jugs" is an example of an imperfect pangram in English.

Because the *Iroha* contains every sound once, it's a perfect choice for helping children to remember the hiragana.

Intriguingly, the *Iroha* was first written in Chinese characters, and was only later adopted as a memory aid for the hiragana. The Chinese text was as follows:

以呂波耳本部止
千利奴流乎和加
餘多連曽津祢那
良牟有為能於久
耶万計不己衣天
阿佐伎喩女美之
恵比毛勢須

ABC SUTRA • ABCスートラ

Later, when it was written in old hiragana, the *Iroha* looked like this*:

いろはにほへと
ちりぬるを
わかよたれそ
つねならむ
うゐのおくやま
けふこえて
あさきゆめみし
ゑひもせす

> Wondering about the words of this poem? Originally attributed to the Buddhist monk *Kuukai*, it's now thought to have been written later, possibly as a tribute to *Kuukai*. Here's one translation:

* Wondering about ゐ and ゑ? Check page 168!

Even the blossoming flowers will eventually scatter.
Who in our world is unchanging?
The deep mountains of karma—we cross them today.
And we shall not have superficial dreams, nor be deluded.

Amazingly, the original Chinese text of the Iroha appears to contain a hidden message. Look at the last character of each line—they form this phrase:

止加那久天之須
Toka nakute shisu.
"Die without wrong-doing."

Some historians believe that this is a eulogy to **Kuukai**, embedded in the poem intentionally to honor him. •

こんにち何?
KONNICHI WHAT?

Why do you say 今日は *konnichi wa* for "good day" when "today" is normally read as 今日 *kyou*?

今日 is an example of a phenomenon that pops up with certain kanji: they have one reading for informal speech, and another for formal speech.

In the case of 今日, the common reading is **きょう *kyou***, and the formal reading is **こんにち *konnichi***. (Both mean "today".)

> The common reading is the native Japanese reading, known as the ***kun-yomi***. The formal reading is the Sino-Japanese reading, known as the ***on-yomi***.*

* For more on this, see page 136.

Here are two more examples:

昨日 'yesterday'
きのう *kinou* (common)
さくじつ *sakujitsu* (formal)

今年 'this year'
ことし *kotoshi* (common)
こんねん *konnen* (formal)

> As for **konnichi wa**, why would one of the most common expressions of all use a formal reading?

> It probably has to do with the fact that **konnichi wa** comes from a longer and much older phrase meaning "how are you feeling today?" •

ロシアより塩を込めて
FROM RUSSIA WITH SALT

I've heard that いくら *ikura* ('salted salmon roe') isn't a native Japanese word. Is that true?

Correct! It's a loan word from Russian.

> When written in katakana, *ikura* looks very Japanese. However, it actually comes from the Russian word *ikra*, meaning 'caviar'.

 'Roe' are the individual mature eggs, which are a commonly-eaten delicacy in both Russia and Japan. They are often thought of as a very Japanese food, and that probably contributes to people assuming *ikura* is a Japanese word. •

バイキングのバイキング
AT THE VIKING BUFFET

Why do I sometimes feel like I'm hearing English words when I listen to Japanese people speaking?

It might be 和製英語 *waseieigo*, which means 'Made-in-Japan English'.

Japanese has borrowed many words from English. Sometimes the word takes on the same meaning in Japanese. Other times, the meaning is related, but not the same. And sometimes, there's no obvious connection at all.

> Flip the page and let's take a look at a few of the strangest (and most entertaining) examples . . .

AT THE VIKING BUFFET • バイキングのバイキング

コンセント *konsento*
From: 'consent'
Japanese meaning: 'electrical outlet'

バイキング *baikingu*
From: 'viking'
Japanese meaning: 'buffet'

ロードショー *roudo shou*
From: 'roadshow'
Japanese meaning:
  'general release (of a film)'

ホッチキス *hocchikisu*
From: 'Hotchkiss'
Japanese meaning: 'stapler'

> Actually, the Hotchkiss was a brand-name stapler, named for its American inventor B.B. Hotchkiss at the start of the 1900's . . .

... so, like the word 'Kleenex' in English, there's a certain logic to that one—though it's quite obscure.

 Obscure? I bet that makes it your favourite!

Actually, my favourite is *baikingu*, because the image of—

 Okay thanks! Anyway, *waseieigo* can also give you a new cultural perspective on a familiar concept.

Take a look at the list on the next page for some examples!

AT THE VIKING BUFFET • バイキングのバイキング

サービス *saabisu*
From: "service"
Japanese meaning: 'on the house'

リサイクルショップ *risaikuru shoppu*
From: "recycle shop"
Japanese meaning: 'second-hand shop'

タレント *tarento*
From: "talent"
Japanese meaning: 'TV personality'

ライブ *raibu*
From: "live"
Japanese meaning: 'show, concert'

プロモーションビデオ (PV) *puromoushon bideo*
From: "promotional video"
Japanese meaning: 'music video'

グラマー *guramaa*
From: "glamour"
Japanese meaning: 'voluptuous'

> My favourites are the ones where the meaning is close, but . . . not quite right:

トランプ *toranpu*
Origin: "trump"
Japanese meaning: 'playing-cards'

ハイテンション *haitenshon*
Origin: "hi-tension"
Japanese meaning: 'energetic'

プレーガイド *puree gaido*
Origin: "play guide"
Japanese meaning: 'box office'

AT THE VIKING BUFFET • バイキングのバイキング

スマート sumaato
From: "smart"
Japanese meaning: 'cool, stylish'
　　　　...*also:* 'thin, slender'

シール shiiru
From: "seal"
Japanese meaning: 'sticker'

Finally, there are times where, even though the word came from English, it refers to something uniquely Japanese.

For example, **OVA** *oubiiee*, which comes from the English phrase "original video animation", but refers specifically to a direct-to-video release of an animated film or series—of which there are many in Japan. •

IT'S QUIZ TIME!

Contestants, get ready! I know you love *waseieigo*, so how about a quiz?

I'll give you a list of *waseieigo*, along with their English origins. Let's see if you can guess the new meanings in Japanese!

Ready? Turn that page!

ロスト・イン・トランスレーション
LOST IN TRANSLATION

> Guess the meaning in Japanese!

1. シャープペンシル *shaapu penshiru*
   (from "sharp pencil")

2. バージョンアップ *baajon appu*
   (from "version up")

3. フリーダイヤル *furii daiyaru*
   (from "free dial")

4. トレーナー *toreenaa*
   (from "trainer")

5. カンニング *kanningu*
   (from "cunning")

6. スマート *sumaato*
   (from "smart")

7 モーニングコール　mouningu kouru
(from "morning call")

8 サラリーマン　sararii man
(from "salary man")

9 オーダーメード　oudaa meedo
(from "order made")

10 テレビゲーム　terebi geemu
(from "TV game")

Answers:
1. mechanical pencil
2. upgrade (e.g. computer software)
3. toll-free call
4. sweatshirt
5. copying (someone else's answer), cheating
6. slim or stylish
7. wake-up call
8. (white-collar) employee
9. custom-made
10. video game

DON'T BE SO CONTRADICTORY

Wherein David explains some of the strangest contradictions of the Japanese language.

Blue Means Go. 90
All My Friend. 94
Brown Means Tea 96
I Hate Not Losing! 98
Crimson Means Red 99
The Evolution Of Wa. 102
Being Contradictory 107

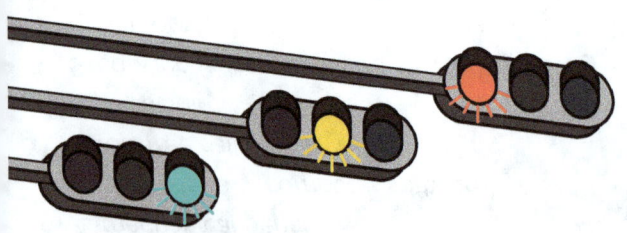

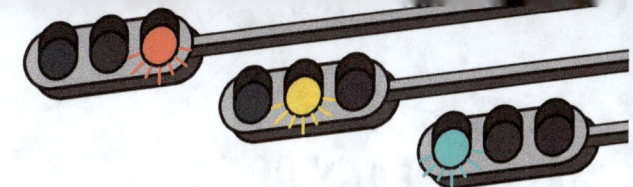

それ、矛盾してない?!

「なんでこんな言い方するの??」にデビットがお答えします!

青で進め! 90
友達はひとりじゃない! 94
お茶はブラウン 96
負けたい! 98
本当に赤でしょう? 99
「わ」の進化 102
矛か盾。どっち?! 107

青で進め!
BLUE MEANS GO

Why are green traffic signals called 青信号 *aoshingou* ('blue traffic light'), when the colour of the signal is obviously green?

For most of the history of Japanese, green was considered a shade of blue.

Although modern Japanese has 緑 *midori* as a distinct word for 'green', this word is a recent development. Educational materials which distinguished green and blue only came into use after World War II.

> In fact, Japanese speakers now use separate words for 藍 *ai* ('navy blue' or 'indigo'), 緑 *midori* ('green'), and 青 *ao*, which translates most closely as 'blue-green'.

However, 青 *ao* can also be translated as 'fresh' or 'newly-grown'. The blue-green colour represented by 青 *ao* is common to newly-grown plant life.

The Chinese translation of 青 *ao* also has the connotation of freshness, and is often used in Chinese for a light blue colour.

Here's how you might use each of the colour words:

藍色のジーンズ *aiiro jiinzu* ('blue jeans')

緑の葉っぱ *midori no happa* ('green leaf')

青信号 *aoshingou* ('green traffic light')

BLUE MEANS GO • 青で進め！

There's an interesting pattern among the four "native" colours in Japanese:

赤い *akai* red
青い *aoi* blue
白い *shiroi* white
黒い *kuroi* black

These four adjectives, which all end with the *-i* inflection い, can connect directly to the word they're describing, without needing any extra words in between.

For example:

赤い靴がかっこいい
Akai kutsu ga kakkoii.
Red shoes look cool.

Meanwhile, look at these colours:

緑　*midori*　green

紫　*murasaki* purple/violet

黄色 *kiiro*　yellow

灰色 *haiiro*　grey ('ash colour')

茶色 *chairo*　brown

ピンク*pinku*　pink

None of these adjectives end with い, and they all require the connecting word の *no* to describe the word after them. For example:

ピンクのリボンが流行ってる
Pinku no ribon ga hayatteru.
Pink ribbons are in style. •

友達はひとりじゃない！
ALL MY FRIEND

In 友達 *tomodachi* ('friend'), the kanji character 達 *tachi* refers to a group. So why is it that only one friend is still called a 友達 *tomodachi*?

There are two common theories. The first theory is that 達 *tachi* doesn't just refer to actual groups, but also to the abstract concept of a group.

> Even when you're only talking about one friend, that person still belongs to your group!

The other theory is based on the second definition for 達 *tachi* given in the Koujien (the primary encyclopedia of the Japanese language).

This definition says that 達 *tachi* can be used as an honourific* to indicate respect.

So, rather than focusing on the idea that a friend is someone in 'your group', this theory focuses on the idea that your friends are people you give respect to.

You can also refer to a single friend as 友人 *yuujin*—but only in formal contexts. •

* An honourific is a title that you attach to a person's name. Two common examples in English are 'Ms.' and 'Doctor'. A well-known example in Japanese is the suffix *-san*.

お茶はブラウン
BROWN MEANS TEA

Given that お茶 *ocha* ('tea') is typically green in Japan, why is the colour brown described as 茶色 *chairo* ('tea colour')?

茶色 *chairo* originally referred to the colour of tea leaves. Most tea leaves turn brown as they dry. So, you can see how 'tea colour' might become a name for the colour brown.

> Even though お茶 *ocha* now typically refers to green tea (*maccha*), keep in mind that green tea was actually introduced to Japan much later than the coarser brown teas. By that time, the use of 茶色 *chairo* ('tea colour') for the colour brown was already widespread.

If you liked that, this will really blow your mind...

...what do you think black tea is called in Japanese?

It's called 紅茶 *koucha*, and the 紅 *kou* means "crimson red". This is because black tea is actually a deep red when brewed.

 So, let's review here... the word for brown in Japanese is "tea colour", even though most Japanese tea is green... and the word for black tea uses the kanji for "red"?

Now you're thinking in Japanese! •

負けず嫌い!
I HATE NOT LOSING!

Why does 負けず嫌い *makezugirai* mean 'to hate losing'? I thought ず *zu* makes a verb negative, which would give the meaning 'to hate *not* losing'?

In this case the ず *zu* is actually short for むず *muzu*, a suffix from the Heian period (794-1185) that means 'speculation'.

This is similar to だろう *darou*. You might translate it as 'hating even the thought of losing'.

When you see ず *zu* elsewhere, it's usually safe to assume it means the same thing as ない *nai*, which also makes verbs negative. •

本当に赤でしょう?
CRIMSON MEANS RED

Why is the first kanji character for the 紅白歌合戦 *kouhaku utagassen* ('red-and-white year-end song festival') written as 紅 *kou* ('crimson'), when it should be 赤 *aka* ('red')?

This is one of those things that native Japanese speaker just accept, even though it's contradictory. Despite being written as the "crimson-and-white" festival, everyone knows it's the Red-and-White Festival.

> Keep in mind that in Japanese, 赤 *aka* ('red') is only used for pure red. Meanwhile, 紅 *kou* ('crimson') is considered an impure shade of red, and is also used for dyed materials.

デビット・ベネット DAVID BENNETT

CRIMSON MEANS RED • 本当に赤でしょう？

The distinction might be a little confusing for English-speakers. Here are two words that will help make it clear:

紅葉 *kouyou*

"Deep red leaves"—meaning 'autumn leaves' or 'autumn colours'.

赤字 *akaji*

"Red writing"—meaning an accounting deficit, like "in the red" in English.

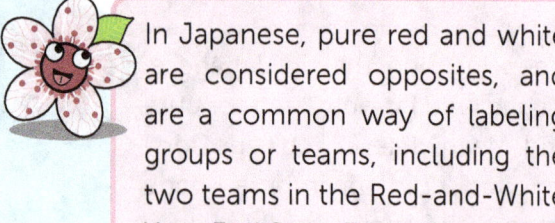

In Japanese, pure red and white are considered opposites, and are a common way of labeling groups or teams, including the two teams in the Red-and-White Year-End Song Festival.

 They're also the colours of celebration. For example, red-and-white banners are used at entrance ceremonies and graduation.

Unfortunately, a quick image search makes it obvious that the distinction between crimson, scarlet, and vermillion is completely lost on most people.

Nope, sorry, 紅 *kou* ('crimson') is *not* simply a more poetic way of saying 赤 *aka* ('red')!

What would be a more poetic way of saying "pedantic"? •

「わ」の進化
THE EVOLUTION OF WA

Why is は *ha* pronounced *wa* when it's used as a topic marker* in sentences like 私は *watashi wa* ('as for me . . .')?

This is one of the many Japanese spelling quirks that survived the spelling reforms of 1946.

> If all you wanted was a simple answer, you can stop here. But if you want my respect, you'll keep reading, *kouhai*.

---

* The concept of the topic marker only exists in a few languages. It's a way to indicate the 'topic' of a sentence, which is the person or thing being *spoken about*. This may be the same as or different from the 'subject', which is the person or thing *doing the action*.

Japanese spelling is intended to show accurate pronunciation. However, it's natural for the pronunciation of a language to shift over time. When this happens, the spelling needs to be updated, to avoid it becoming disconnected from the pronunciation.

In 1946, Japanese spelling, which had become archaic and confusing, was reformed to match current pronunciation.

At that time, the topic marker は *ha* was being pronounced as *wa*. Rather than change the written topic marker to わ *wa* to reflect the pronunciation, which would have made numerous written texts obsolete, the topic marker は *ha* was exempted from the spelling reform.

>>>

THE EVOLUTION OF WA • 「わ」の進化

(There were two other exemptions. The first is the direction/destination marker へ *e*, which would normally be pronounced *he*. The second is を *o*, which is used to mark the object of a verb. を *o* was once pronounced *wo* and had other uses, but is now used only for marking objects.)

As a result of this exemption, Japanese people continue to write は *ha* while saying *wa*, even though the rest of Japanese spelling is mostly phonemic.*

---

* Phonemic spelling means that the spelling of a word corresponds directly to the way you say it. English spelling is *not* phonemic. For example, the letter 'c' can represent either an "s" sound or a "k" sound in English.

は

> Fascinating, isn't it? But if you want the full story, we have to go all the way back to 800 BC . . .

> Why, are you going to share a memory from your childhood?

In Old Japanese, は was pronounced with a "p" sound—*pa*.

Over time, the "p" sound changed into an "f" sound. We know this because early Portuguese records of pre-modern Japanese use "f" to record the sound, rather than "p" or "h".

The sound kept changing, and nowadays is somewhere between "f" and "h" to the ears of an English-speaker. (Although ふ *fu* stayed closer to an "f" sound.)

>>>

THE EVOLUTION OF WA • 「わ」の進化

When the "f/h" sound appears in the middle of a word, such as it does in a verb like 買う (Old Japanese: 買フ *kafu*, but then pronounced *kapu*), it's either pronounced with a "w" sound, or dropped entirely. (For example, this gives *kau* and *kawanai* rather than *kapu* and *kapanai*.)

The same thing happened to the topic marker は *ha*, which came to be pronounced *wa*.

> And now you know the real story of how *pa* became *fa* became *ha* became *wa* in spoken Japanese . . . but continues to be written with は *ha*, one of the few exceptions in Japanese spelling today. •

矛か盾。どっち?!
BEING CONTRADICTORY

. . . where's Kuizu? Isn't it time for our chapter-ending quiz?

Nope!!

I don't get it, why not?

He's being . . . contradictory.

「なにヤニさがってんの?!」

> You're in *my* house now!

PRECISE DISTINCTIONS

A Precise River 110
Asking Precisely 112
Precisely Lying Down 114
This Is A Hard One. 116
A Precise Beard 119
Harbouring Differences 120
What About Dancing Shrimp? 122
Sai vs. Sai. 124
Precisely Vague 127

任せろ！

厳密に言えば

(細) 川 110
きく？きく。 112
(細) 横になる 114
これはハード 116
(細) ヒゲ 119
天気予報 120
踊っているエビって何？ 122
歳・才 124
少年よ、「曖昧」を抱け 127

デビット・ベネット DAVID BENNETT

(細)川
A PRECISE RIVER

The kanji characters 川 *kawa*, 河 *kawa*, and 江 *e* all mean 'river'. What's the difference?

Most Japanese speakers today only use the modern form, 川 *kawa*.

> . . . Which is downright criminal, considering the nuances of meaning and history that are lost by such laziness.

> Nah, you don't really need to worry about the differences for everyday use.

The precise (historical) meanings of the three forms *are* fascinating, though!

川 *kawa* refers to a big river, and was originally used to refer to rivers in Japan.

河 *kawa* refers to a big and meandering river, and was originally used to refer to rivers in Korea.

江 *e* or *kou* refers to very long rivers spanning entire regions, and was originally used to refer to rivers in China.

> 江 *kou* is also used for salt water areas, like inlets, and for anywhere that water meets land. •

きく？きく。
ASKING PRECISELY

What's the difference between the three homonyms* 聞く *kiku*, 聴く *kiku*, and 訊く *kiku*?

There are many homonyms in Japanese, but 聞く *kiku*, 聴く *kiku*, and 訊く *kiku* are especially difficult. Their meanings are different, but related, so it's easy to mix them up.

- 聞く means either 'to hear something incidentally' or 'to ask'.
- 聴く means 'to listen intently'.
- 訊く means 'to ask'.

---

* Homonyms are words that sound the same, or are spelled the same, but have different meanings.

Nowadays, Japanese writers typically use 聞く *kiku* to refer to all of these meanings, but you'll still see the other forms in some written materials.

> If you want to express the verb 'ask' in Japanese, there's no difference between 聞く *kiku* and 訊く *kiku*, except that 聞く *kiku* is more common. •

(細) 横になる
PRECISELY LYING DOWN

What's the difference between 腹這い *harabai* and うつ伏せ *utsubuse*, since both of them mean 'to lie face down'?

While both mean 'to lie face down', 腹這い *harabai* implies that your eyes are open and you are awake, whereas うつ伏せ *utsubuse* implies that your eyes are closed (regardless of whether you are asleep). Therefore, うつ伏せ *utsubuse* carries more of a connotation of relaxing.

> If you want to be really precise (which you do), you should also know the verbs 寝る *neru* ('to lie down', 'to sleep lying down') and 眠る *nemuru* ('to sleep', but not necessarily lying down).

Here are examples of how you might hear 腹這い *harabai* and うつ伏せ *utsubuse* in normal use:

腹這いで進め!
Harabai de susume!
Move forward in a crawl!

マッサージをするのでうつ伏せになって下さい
Massaaji wo suru node, utsubuse ni natte kudasai.
Please lie face-down, as it's time for your massage.

Was Bento talking earlier? I feel a sudden urge to 眠る *nemuru*.

これはハード
THIS IS A HARD ONE

What's up with the kanji characters 固い, 堅い, and 硬い? They're all read as *katai* and they all seem to mean 'hard' or 'solid'. What's the difference?

With a more nuanced translation, the differences become clear:

- 硬い means 'hard', the opposite of 'soft'.

- 堅い means 'durable' or 'solid', the opposite of 'fragile'.

- 固い means 'firm', the opposite of 'wavering' or 'movable'.

> The final character, 固い *katai*, is generally used to describe a state of mind. For example:

頭が固い *atama ga katai* ('stubborn')

頑固 *ganko* (also 'stubborn')

固く信じる *kataku shinjiru* ('strongly or fervently believe')

> To help you remember the difference, you can try pairing up each *katai* character with a word that has the opposite meaning:

A rock is 硬い *katai* . . .
. . . a pillow is 柔らかい *yawarakai* ('soft')

A well-built building is 堅い *katai* . . .
. . . a vase is 脆い *moroi* ('fragile')

A person who refuses to compromise is 固い *katai* . . .
. . . someone who backs down easily is 素直 *sunao* ('obedient, meek')

>>>

THIS IS A HARD ONE • これはハード

> Don't forget that each character has some additional meanings that add nuance:

- 硬い can also mean 'unpolished writing'.
- 堅い can also mean 'stuffy writing' or 'honourable'.
- 固い can also mean 'certain' or 'solemn'. •

(細) ヒゲ
A PRECISE BEARD

What's the difference between the three kanji characters (髭・髯・鬚) for *hige*? Don't they all just mean 'facial hair'?

No, there are slight differences:

髭 means 'facial hair around the mouth'.

髯 means 'facial hair on the cheeks'.

鬚 means 'facial hair on the chin'.

> The first character, 髭 *hige* ('facial hair around the mouth'), is also used for complete beards. •

天気予報
HARBOURING DIFFERENCES

What's the difference between a 津波 *tsunami* and a tidal wave?

Although 津波 *tsunami* literally translates as 'harbour wave', it's now used by both English and Japanese speakers to refer to a wave caused by geologic forces—earthquake, volcanic eruption, coastal landslide, or even a meteor strike.

> When an English speaker says "tidal wave", there are a couple of things they might mean.

> Sometimes they mean a *tsunami* as described above. Other times, they just mean the normal waves of the tide, caused by the gravity of the moon and sun.

But, most properly, 'tidal wave' is a synonym of 'tidal bore'.

A tidal bore is a phenomenon where the tide enters a long and narrow inlet, is compressed into a larger and stronger wave, and then flows upstream, against the current of the river.

In Japanese, a tidal bore is called a 海嘯 *kaishou*.

踊っているエビって何?
WHAT ABOUT DANCING SHRIMP?

The kanji characters 海老 *ebi* and 蝦 *ebi* both seem to mean 'shrimp'. What's the difference?

Simple! 海老 *ebi* is used for shrimp that walk, while 蝦 *ebi* is used for shrimp that swim.

The distinction probably seems unnecessary, but consider that English uses the words 'prawn' and 'shrimp' to make an equally unnecessary distinction based on size and number of claws.

舞踏会はどこでしょうか?

Nowadays, the kanji character 蝦 *ebi* is rarely used, as Japanese speakers aren't too concerned with whether their food used to walk or swim—just as many English speakers wouldn't be able to tell you the difference between a prawn and a shrimp. •

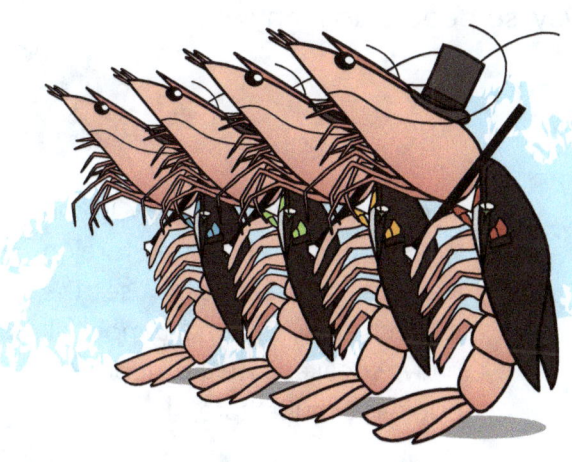

歳・才
SAI VS. SAI

I thought the correct kanji for 'age' was 歳 *sai*, but I always see native Japanese speakers writing it as 才 *sai*. What's up?

It saves time.

No, seriously! This is one of those instances where something is incorrect, but it's much easier than the "correct" way, so people do it anyway.

Lazy!

The result is pretty funny if you think about it. Almost all foreign learners of Japanese use the correct kanji, 歳, and almost all native speakers use the incorrect-but-easier substitute, 才.

To be clear, the meanings of these two kanji characters aren't related at all. 才 *sai* refers to ability, talent, or aptitude, and has nothing to do with age.

The reason for using 才 *sai* is simply that it sounds like 歳 *sai*, so it saves effort while still getting the meaning across. Here's an example common in Japan:

> 6才でいい年ですね
> 6*sai de ii toshi desune.*
> Six years old is a great age.

The correct form, requiring an additional ten strokes, would be:

> 6歳でいい年ですね

If you ask me, ten strokes is a small price to pay to be correct!

IT'S QUIZ TIME!

Contestants, get ready! Some words in Japanese are very precise, while others have so many meanings it's impossible to keep track of them all!

In this quiz, I'll give you some words with a lot of strange meanings, some real, some made up. Let's see if you can guess which meanings are *not* the real ones!

少年よ、「曖昧」を抱け
PRECISELY VAGUE

---

1. Which of the following are NOT real meanings of こうか *kouka*?

- **A** engineering course
- **B** crimson mist
- **C** school song
- **D** indestructible mecha robot
- **E** toilet
- **F** gelatinization
- **G** marriage of an Imperial princess to one of her subjects
- **H** flabby lips
- **I** conversion to fiber optics
- **J** taxes
- **K** soup made with at least two kinds of turnip
- **L** world-destroying conflagration

Answer: D, H, and K are not real meanings of kouka. Believe it or not, the rest are all real!

>>>

デビット・ベネット DAVID BENNETT

PRECISELY VAGUE • 少年よ、「曖昧」を抱け

2. Which of the following are NOT real meanings of こうし *koushi*?

- **A** crystal lattice
- **B** small cow
- **C** large cow
- **D** to exercise one's authority
- **E** photon
- **F** pearly white teeth
- **G** blackened teeth
- **H** arrow to which is attached a turnip-shaped whistle made of hollowed-out wood or deer horn, the whistling of which is used to signal the start of battle
- **I** hind leg
- **J** jade sculpture
- **K** pre-war school for male teachers

Answer: C, G, and J are not real meanings of *koushi*. The rest are real! (Yes, even the arrow with the whistling turnip-thing!)

3. Which of the following are NOT real meanings of やく *yaku*?

- **A** formula 1 racing
- **B** approximately
- **C** yakuza (the Japanese mafia)
- **D** burn a CD or DVD
- **E** shortening
- **F** the time in a person's life when they are too old to enjoy being childish, but too young to be financially established
- **G** to feel jealous
- **H** drugs
- **I** strawberry juice
- **J** bad luck
- **K** a role one plays, on stage or in society
- **L** a yak

Answer: A, C, F, and I are not real meanings of yaku. The rest are real!

>>>

PRECISELY VAGUE • 少年よ、「曖昧」を抱け

4. Which of the following are NOT real meanings of the verb きる *kiru*?

- **A** to bear guilt
- **B** to taunt a bear or other large animal
- **C** to turn off a light
- **D** to punch a ticket
- **E** to power up a mecha
- **F** to act decisively
- **G** to shuffle cards
- **H** to dig a groove
- **I** to drop a breakable object
- **J** to let something drain
- **K** to start
- **L** to hang up a phone
- **M** to contemplate one's place in society
- **N** to open somethig that was sealed

Answer: B, E, I, and M are not real meanings of kiru. The rest are!

5. Which of the following are NOT real meanings of うつる utsuru?

- **A** to be reflected in something, or to be reflected by something
- **B** to suffer an emotionally crushing defeat due to one's own incompetence
- **C** to harmonize with
- **D** to marry an Imperial princess [used when speaking about a commoner]
- **E** to be permeated by a colour or scent
- **F** to be contagious
- **G** to travel faster than the speed of sound
- **H** to move to a new home
- **I** to be host to a parasite

Answer: B, D, G, and I are not real meanings of yaku. The rest are! With thanks to the excellent Twitter account @Nihomophones—follow them for more fun with the Japanese language!

デビット・ベネット DAVID BENNETT

KANJI PANIC 2: REVENGE OF KANJI

Wherein we unravel some of the mysterious meanings of kanji characters.

Both Fists Bump?................134
Jumping Birds?..................135
It's Pronounced "Confusing".......136
Sunday Again??..................140
Kanji in a Box..................144
It's Windy Up Here!.............150
Sometimes It Takes A Lot........153
...And Sometimes A Little.......156
Which Country??.................159

漢字パニック2:
ザ・リベンジ

漢字の不思議を探ろう!

フィストバンプ? 134
鳥のジャンプ? 135
同じ漢字、違う発音 136
「日」ってすごい 140
説文解字 144
風が強い! 150
意外と言いにくい 153
意外と言いやすい 156
漢字圏の国 159

デビット・ベネット DAVID BENNETT

フィストバンプ？
BOTH FISTS BUMP?

What are the kanji characters for 'rock, paper, scissors'?

The kanji characters for the game 'rock, paper, scissors' are 両拳碰 *jankenpon*. The literal translations are:

両 'both'   拳 'fists'   碰 'chance' or 'bump'

Interestingly, the hand gestures are still a fist, an open palm, and two fingers. And despite the translation of 両拳碰 *jankenpon*, Japanese people do interpret those hand gestures as a rock, a piece of paper, and scissors.

So, why *jankenpon*? Because the characters 両拳碰 describe the movements of the game, rather than the 'weapons' being used.

鳥のジャンプ？
JUMPING BIRDS?

When a ski jumper launches off the ramp, they are said to とぶ *tobu*. Which kanji characters do you use for *tobu*? Should it be 飛ぶ *tobu* ('to fly'), or 跳ぶ *tobu* ('to jump')?

For ski jumping, it's 飛ぶ *tobu* ('to fly').

> In general, 飛ぶ *tobu* ('to fly') means to fly with wings, or to soar through the air. 跳ぶ *tobu* ('to jump') means to launch yourself into the air using your legs and feet.

> However, some linguists argue that since ski jumpers push off with their legs, we should use 跳ぶ *tobu* ('to jump') instead. •

デビット・ベネット DAVID BENNETT

同じ漢字、違う発音
IT'S PRONOUNCED "CONFUSING"

Why does a single kanji often have more than one reading*?

The readings of kanji characters come from many sources and time periods.

Keep in mind that kanji characters were adopted from China. As a result, there are two main origins for the readings of a kanji character:

音読み *on-yomi* ('sino-Japanese reading') refers to a pronunciation that is based on the original Chinese pronunciation of the character.

訓読み *kun-yomi* ('native reading') refers to a pronunciation that comes from the

---

* A "reading" is one way of saying the kanji character out loud.

traditional Japanese word that has the same meaning as the kanji character.

Most kanji characters have at least one *on-yomi* and one *kun-yomi*.

> Of course, if that were as complicated as things got, we wouldn't be having this conversation.

Some kanji characters crossed over to Japan more than once, during different eras of Chinese history. These characters ended up with different *on-yomi* from each time they crossed over.

> In fact, you can classify 音読み *on-yomi* based on three major eras in the history of the Chinese language:

>>>

IT'S PRONOUNCED "CONFUSING" • 同じ漢字、違う発音

呉音 *go on* ('Wu sound') refers to the pronunciation from the Southern and Northern Dynasties in the 5th–6th centuries. (The Wu region is now Shanghai.)

漢音 *kan on* ('Han sound') refers to the pronunciation during the Tang Dynasty in the 7th–9th centuries, coming mainly from the speech of the capital *Chang'an* (which today is *Xi'an*).

唐音 *tou on* ('Tang sound') refers to the pronunciation from the later Song and Ming dynasties*, and covers all the readings adopted from the Heian era through to the Edo period (10th–19th centuries).

* Yes, the Tang sound really did come from the Song and Ming Dynasties, and yes, the Han sound came from the Tang Dynasty. Chinese history is complicated!

Here are some kanji characters that have several **on-yomi**:

		go-on	*kan-on*	*tou-on*
明	bright	myou	mei	min *
行	go	gyou/gou	kyou/kou	an *
極	extreme	goku	kyoku	-
珠	pearl	shu	shu	ju
度	degree	do	to *	-
子	child	shi	shi	su
清	clear	shou	sei	shin *
京	capital	kyou	kei	kin *
兵	soldier	hyou	hei	-
強	strong	gou	kyou	-

* uncommon or rare reading

One more: 慣用音 *kan-you-on* ('excepted pronunciations') are mistaken or changed readings of kanji characters. •

「日」ってすごい
SUNDAY AGAIN??

Are there any examples of kanji with a *lot* of different readings or meanings?

The kanji 上 has six very distinct readings: うえ *ue*, うわ *uwaa*, かみ *kami*, あげる *aageru*, のぼる *nobouru*, and ジョウ *jou*.

> It also has a Brobdingnagian list of meanings, all of which derive from the broad concepts of 'up', 'before', and 'superior'.

For the character 上 alone (not including any compounds), the meanings include:

- on top of, on, above, up, over
- "from the standpoint of . . . ", "as a matter of . . . ", "as concerns . . . "
- first volume (e.g. of a book)
- superior quality, best, top, high class

- going up (e.g. elevator)
- aboard (e.g. ship or vehicle)
- governmental, imperial, emperor, sovereign, shogun
- summit, surface, top
- before, previous
- superiority, one's superior or elder
- "in addition", "what's more", "upon further inspection", "besides"
- "based on . . . ", "following from . . . ", "because", "since", "for that reason"
- upper reaches (of a river)
- long ago, beginning, first
- head of the table

Whew! Now, how about using one kanji to form a lot of different words? Got anything Bento?

SUNDAY AGAIN?? • 「日」ってすごい

Check out this two-sentence beauty based on the kanji 日!

3月1日は日曜日で祝日。
日本は晴れの日です

Sangatsu tsuitachi ha nichiyoubi de shukujitsu. Nihon ha hare no hi desu.

March 1st* is holiday Sunday.
It is a sunny day in Japan**.

---

* The 日 here doesn't exactly mean '1st'. Rather, the whole word *tsuitachi* means "first-day", with 日 meaning 'day'. There's no way to highlight 'day' in English, since we write '1st'.

** *Nihon* means "sun's origin" (referring to Japan being east of China). The 日 *ni* in *Nihon* is the word for 'sun', but there's no way to highlight *ni* in the English name 'Japan'.

That's 日 used six times in two sentences to form five different words! The six instances of 日 are:

- 日 たち *tachi*
- 日 にち *nichi*
- 日 び *bi*
- 日 じつ *jitsu*
- 日 に *ni*
- 日 ひ *hi*

All six instances of 日 have the same meaning, 'sun' or 'day'. (The two ideas are closely related in Japanese.) Five words are formed: 'holiday', 'Sunday', 'day', 'Japan' (**Nihon**), and 'first-day' (first of the month).

> If you look closely, even the kanji 晴 *hare* 'sunny' is formed with 日 as one of its components! •

説文解字
KANJI IN A BOX

Kanji characters seem to have so many different origins. Pictures, sounds, compounds . . . how can I keep it all straight?

Keep in mind that kanji characters were originally Chinese writing. They came to Japan more than a thousand years ago, and their meaning and pronunciation has evolved ever since. Trying to fit them into any simple system would be impossible.

However, there is a traditional system for classifying Chinese characters. Although considered outdated and imperfect today, it still offers insight into some of the possible origins of kanji characters.

> Just remember that this isn't any sort of official classification.

There are six categories in the traditional classification of Chinese characters:

象形文字 *shoukei moji*
These characters are simply a drawing of whatever object they represent. (This is also known as a pictogram.)

- 木　　*ki* 'tree'
- 日　　*hi* 'sun'

指事文字 *shiji moji*
These characters are a representation of an abstract concept. (This is also known as an ideograph.)

- 上　　*ue* 'up'
- 下　　*shita* 'down'

>>>

KANJI IN A BOX • 説文解字

会意文字 *kaii moji*

These are combinations of pictograms that, taken together, produce a new meaning.

休 *yasu/yasumu* 'rest'

This combines a person (人 *hito*, in a simplified form) with a tree (木 *ki*). This gives a person leaning against a tree, resting.

形声文字 *keisei moji*

These compounds account for 90% of all kanji. They combine two components. Usually, but by no means always, the one at the top or left suggests the general category or idea, and the other component approximates the pronunciation. (These are known as phono-semantic or radical-phonetic compounds.)

This category is hard to apply to kanji, because the pronunciation hint refers to the Chinese reading of the character, rather than the native Japanese reading.

For example:

 go 'language'

The left-hand side, 言 *gon*, means 'speak', and hints that the character relates to speaking.

The right-hand side, 吾 *go*, indicates the sound.

The full meaning of 語 *go* ('language') can be seen in the word 日本語 *nihongo* 'Japanese language'.

転注文字 *tenchuu moji*

This is a vaguely-defined category that refers to a kanji where the meaning has become extended. For example:

 *raku* 'comfort', 'ease'

The word 音楽 *ongaku* 'music' extends the meaning of this character.

仮借文字 *kasha moji*

Another vague category, for characters that began with one of the origins above but have present-day meanings that are unrelated. For example:

In ancient Chinese, this was a pictograph for wheat. By coincidence, it sounded the same as the verb 'to come'.

Over time, the character has taken on the meaning 'to come' instead of the original meaning 'wheat'. For example, in 来る *kuru* 'to come' or 'to return'.

> You aren't going to believe this next part. (But it's true!)

The character 麦 *mugi* 'wheat' originally meant . . . 'to come'. It was a phono-semantic compound, with 'foot' at the bottom to suggest the meaning, and the top character suggesting the sound. However, the top character was (you guessed it) 'wheat', and it eventually took on that meaning instead.

In other words, the characters 来 and 麦 managed to swap meanings! •

風が強い！
IT'S WINDY UP HERE!

Why is it written 台風 *taifuu* ('typhoon'), if 台 *dai* means 'pedestal' or 'stand'?

The kanji character 台 *dai* is actually the simplified form of 颱 *tai*, which means 'typhoon' in Chinese.

If you'd only heard the word *taifuu* spoken aloud, you might guess it was written with the characters 大 *dai* ('big') + 風 *kaze* ('wind'), since this could be sounded as *taifuu*, and seems like it would mean 'big wind'.

> But, in fact, 大風 *taifuu* is a separate word! It refers to a strong gust of wind, not a typhoon.

The original Chinese loan word was actually 颱風 *taifuu*. The literal translation is 'typhoon wind', but the meaning was simply 'typhoon'.

Over time, the Japanese substituted the simplified kanji character 台 *dai* in place of 颱 *tai*, which gave the present-day written form 台風 *taifuu*.

> Around the end of the Meiji period (1868–1912), the character 颱 *tai* was re-introduced to Japan.

> By this time the form 台風 *taifuu* had become standard, so the word never regained the original character 颱 *tai*. It continued to be written as 台風 *taifuu* . . .

IT'S WINDY UP HERE! • 風が強い！

... as a result, the history of the word and its connection to the original character 颱 *tai* are no longer obvious.

To take things a bit further, there's a separate Chinese character 颶 meaning 'hurricane'.

In English, both 'typhoon' and 'hurricane' are synonyms for a tropical cyclone, also known as a cyclonic storm.

Typically, 'hurricane' is used for Atlantic and East Pacific cyclones, while 'typhoon' is used for West Pacific cyclones. •

意外と言いにくい
SOMETIMES IT TAKES A LOT...

Are there any kanji compounds* that have fewer spoken syllables than they have written characters?

Yes there are!

> At first, it seems like this should be impossible, since Japanese characters each represent one or more syllables. So how can you have fewer syllables than characters?

It turns out there are actually two ways these 'impossible compounds' can arise.

* A kanji compound is a word comprising several kanji characters.

SOMETIMES IT TAKES A LOT... • 意外と言いにく

The first way is when a Chinese word has been borrowed into Japanese, and the *kun-yomi* (native Japanese reading of the kanji characters) has fewer syllables than the Chinese word.

The second way is when the spoken word is shortened for convenience, but is still understood to refer to the written word in its full form.

Here are a few simple examples, each with one fewer syllable than the number of kanji characters:

百舌鳥 *mozu* ('shrike')

香具師 *yashi* ('huckster')

今日 *kyou* ('today')

> Note that 海鼠 *ko* is usually read as **namako**, so this is an example of a shortened word.

> Now, here are a couple of my favourites...

<u>山上復有山</u> *ide* means 'the shape of two mountains stacked on top of each other'. Or, translated literally, "on top of one mountain comes another mountain", which is a literary allusion from classical Chinese.

<u>八十一</u> *kuku* means 'eighty-one'. The reading comes from **ku ku**, meaning 'nine times nine', which of course makes eighty-one. •

意外と言いやすい
...AND SOMETIMES A LITTLE

Are there any kanji characters that are spoken aloud as five or more syllables?

Why, yes! Just as some people like to know the longest words in English, many Japanese people know these examples:

- 政 *matsurigoto* ('rule, government')
- 志 *kokorozashi* ('will', 'intention', 'motive')
- 詔 *mikotonori* ('imperial edict')
- 勅 *mikotonori* ('imperial order')
- 承る *uketamawaru* ('to hear', 'to be told', 'to know')

However, there are kanji spoken with as many as seven syllables:

🟡 竓 *miririttoru* ('milliliter')

🟡 竰 *senchirittoru* ('centilitre')

🟡 竡 *hekutorittoru* ('hectolitre')

🟡 粨 *hekutomeetoru* ('hectometer')

🟡 糎 *senchimeetoru* ('centimeter')

🟡 粍 *mirimeetoru* ('millimeter')

🟡 籵 *maikuromeetoru* ('micrometer')

These aren't native Japanese words . . . or even Chinese!

Nope! They're loan words from English. But, they're in common use today, so when it comes to the prize for most syllables, they should probably qualify. •

IT'S QUIZ TIME!

Contestants, get ready! Most country names in Japanese can be written with katakana, like アメリカ *amerika* for America!

But did you know that many countries have *alternate written names* that use kanji characters? It's true!

See if you can guess which countries these kanji characters refer to!

漢字圏の国
WHICH COUNTRY??

See if you can guess which countries these kanji characters refer to!

1. 米国 *beikoku* 'rice country'
2. 英国 *eikoku* 'excellent country'
3. 独国 *dokukoku* 'alone country'
4. 仏国 *fukkoku* 'Buddha country'
5. 豪州 *goushuu* 'powerful province'
6. 土国 *dokoku* 'soil country'
7. 泰国 *taikoku* 'peaceful country'
8. 中国 *chuugoku* 'middle kingdom'

Answers: *1. America 2. England 3. Germany 4. France 5. Australia 6. Turkey 7. Thailand 8. China*

EXPLAIN THIS TO ME

For all those times when you really need to know what a word means... and why.

Trouble At Midnight 162
Respecting Mr. Fuji 163
Too Close to Home 164
Worse Than Two-Faced 166
The Disappearance of Wi 168
Ring, Baby, Ring! 170
Is Ten Minutes Enough? 172
Thank You Is Difficult 173
The Roots of Wasabi 176
Unexpected Trends 179

頼む、教えてくれ！
知ってればお得な言葉

夜の問題 162
「山」は「やま」の時もある 163
細かすぎ 164
裏表があるよりも 166
この文字って何? 168
鳴らせ! 170
十分足りる? 172
サンキューは難しい 173
ワサビの根 176
意外な傾向 179

デビット・ベネット DAVID BENNETT

夜の問題
TROUBLE AT MIDNIGHT

What is the meaning of 夜半 yahan, which is often used in weather reports?

It refers to the hour between 11:30pm and 12:30am.

The origins of 夜半 yahan are quite old, and the term is commonly found in Enka songs (traditional Japanese sentimental ballads).

It refers to the time of night that husbands sneak out to meet their mistresses! •

2:00PM

7:00PM

11:30PM

「山」は「やま」の時もある
RESPECTING MR. FUJI

What does the *san* in 富士山 *fujisan* ('Mt. Fuji') mean?

It means 'mountain'.

> People mistakenly think the *san* is meant to show respect, like adding *-san* to a name.

> In fact, 山 ('mountain') has two readings, *yama* (native Japanese) and *san* (sino-Japanese). This is where *fujisan* really comes from.

> It's said that Japan's three most beautiful mountains are 富士山 *fujisan*, 白山 *hakusan*, and 立山 *tateyama*. (Mt. Fuji, Mt. Haku, and Mt. Tate.) •

細かすぎ
TOO CLOSE TO HOME

What is the meaning of 直下型地震 *chokkagatajishin*?

This is an earthquake with its focus (hypocenter) less than 20km underground. They are particularly devastating and often occur near population centers.

The literal meaning of the word is:

直下	*chokka*	('directly below')
型	*gata*	('type')
地	*ji*	('ground')
震	*shin*	('quake, shake')

> Many dictionaries translate this as 'epicentral earthquake'. This is misleading, since every quake has an epicenter (a point on the surface straight above the focus).

A better translation, seen in some dictionaries, is 'near-field earthquake', emphasizing that the focus is not far underground.

Another term sometimes used in English is 'inland shallow earthquake'.

Unlike most of the earthquakes in Japan, *chokkagatajishin* occur along active fault lines.

The Great Hanshin earthquake of 1995, which devastated the city of Kobe (*Koube*), was this kind of earthquake. •

裏表があるよりも
WORSE THAN TWO-FACED

Why is the Japanese word for turkey 七面鳥 shichimenchou, meaning 'seven-faced bird'?

The common belief is that this refers to the way a turkey's face changes colour depending on its feelings (white, pink, red, purple, and so on).

Unlike North Americans, modern Japanese families don't follow a tradition of eating Turkey at Christmas. Instead, they eat KFC!

In the 1980's, KFC had a very successful marketing campaign that cemented the idea that the perfect Christmas Eve dinner is a bucket of the Colonel's fried chicken!

This is usually eaten along with a "Christmas cake". Unlike many Commonwealth countries, in Japan a Christmas Cake is not a moist fruitcake.

It's just a simple (but delicious!) strawberry shortcake, with "Merry Christmas" written on it.

Some people in Japan also use "Christmas cake" to refer to a woman who's past her prime . . .

DON'T EVEN GO THERE!

この文字って何?
THE DISAPPEARANCE OF WI

The other day I saw a shrine called 京都ゑびす神社 in Kyoto. What the heck is ゑ?

You've discovered a retired character!

> What's his pension like?

From the Kamakura period through the Taishou era (1185–1926), the Japanese language included the sounds *wi*, *we*, and *wo*. These sounds were written as:

	hiragana	katakana
wi	ゐ	ヰ
we	ゑ	ヱ
wo	を	ヲ

You might recognize を as a character you still see commonly today, but which you now pronounce as *o* rather than *wo*.

This is because を has persisted as a way of marking the object of a sentence.*

Meanwhile, ゐ *wi* and ゑ *we* have almost completely disappeared.

> They were formally retired from written Japanese in the spelling reforms of 1946. They're done like dinner!

You can still find them used in older texts, such as the name of 京都ゑびす神社 ***Kyouto webisu jinja*** ('Kyoto Ebisu Shrine').

They also appear in some brand names, such as **ヱビス *Yebisu***, a popular brand of beer produced by Sapporo Breweries. •

---

* For more on this, see "The Evolution Of Wa" on page 102.

鳴らせ!
RING, BABY, RING!

Why are bicycles called チャリンコ *charinko* (frequently shortened to just *chari*)?

The dictionary term for a bicycle in Japanese is actually 自転車 *jitensha* (meaning 'self-powered' + 'wheel' + 'vehicle/car').

チャリンコ *charinko* is a common nickname used around Japan, and there are two suggested origins for the term.

> The most likely explanation is that it comes from the onomatopoeia* for a ringing bell, チャリンチャリン *charincharin*.

* An *onomatopoeia* is a word that imitates a sound. In English, words like 'beep' and 'splash' are onomatopoeias.

By shortening *charincharin* and adding 子 *ko* ('child'), you get チャリンコ *charinko*.

 It's believed that チャリンコ *charinko* first came into popular use in Osaka, after World War II.

Another theory, which is seen as less likely, is that *charinko* comes from the Korean word for bicycle, チャルンケ *charunke*.

 But where's the fun in that? •

十分足りる?
IS TEN MINUTES ENOUGH?

Why can 十分 mean either *jyuppun* ('10 minutes') or *jyuubun* ('enough' or 'plenty')?

The counter* 分 *pun* is used to count minutes, giving *jyuppun* 'ten minutes'. However, it previously meant 'one tenth'.

If you have ten tenths (*jyuubun*), then you have the whole thing, hence the meaning 'enough'.

Here's how you might use *jyuubun* in a sentence:

十分ある! *jyuubun aru!* ('We have enough!')

I think that's *jyuubun*, don't you?

* Counters are explained on page 50.

サンキューは難しい
THANK YOU IS DIFFICULT

Why is the word for 'thank you' sometimes written with kanji characters, 有り難う *arigatou*? And what do the characters mean?

The original phrase for 'thank you' was 「有り難し」 *arigatashi*, which loosely translates to 'existing is difficult'. The idea was that the difficulty of existing led to a sense of appreciation and thankfulness.

The phrase was later reduced to 「有難き」 *arigataki,* and then shortened to 「有難い」 *arigatai*.

The final form, 有り難う *arigatou*, translates literally as 'causing trouble'. This is the form that the hiragana phrase ありがとう *arigatou* comes from.

>>>

デビット・ベネット DAVID BENNETT

THANK YOU IS DIFFICULT • サンキューは難しい

This modern form combines the original meaning of appreciation with the idea of having imposed on someone, or having caused trouble.

> Socially, 有り難う *arigatou* is not the same as 'thank you' in English. 有り難う *arigatou* should only be used when truly thankful or appreciative for something the listener has done, not for small gestures like a held door.

> In that situation, you'd usually say すみません *sumimasen* ('sorry to trouble you' or 'excuse me').

> Most Japanese people also wouldn't use ありがとう *arigatou* in response to a compliment.

> They'd be more likely to humbly disagree—or attempt to change the subject!

The meaning of the word 有難い *arigatai* has changed over time. Around 600–700 AD, the meaning was 'rare', according to the *Manyoushuu* (the oldest existing collection of Japanese poems and legends.)

By 970-1021 AD, two meanings existed. The **Genji Monogatari** (*Tale of Genji*) gives 'hard to live', while **Utsuho Monogatari** (*Tale of the Hollow Tree*) gives 'excellent' or 'splendid', derived from 'rare'.

This was followed by 'to be gracious enough to do something' (derived from 'splendid'). The meaning then shifted to 'thankfulness', and by modern times again to 'a fortunate occurrence'. •

ワサビの根
THE ROOTS OF WASABI

What do the kanji characters for わさび *wasabi* ('Japanese horseradish') mean?

Nowadays, most Japanese people use the hiragana わさび to write the word *wasabi*, rather than the kanji characters, which are 山葵.

山 *yama* means 'mountain', and 葵 *aoi* means 'mallow' or 'asarum' (both being types of plants).

> This makes it sound like wasabi is named 'mountain asarum'. But asarum is actually a different plant entirely! It smells like ginger root, but is toxic—so don't eat it!

Real wasabi is part of the cabbage family, along with mustard and horseradish.

It's also rare in the West, where most products that are labelled "wasabi" are actually a combination of horseradish, mustard, and food colouring, rather than the true wasabi plant.

There's also an older written form for *wasabi*: 和佐比. This series of kanji characters is used for their sounds (*wa* + *sa* + *bi*), rather than for the meanings of the characters. Kanji used in this way are called 当て字 *ateji* ('called-upon characters'). •

IT'S QUIZ TIME!

Contestants, get ready! The Japanese language can be weird, but fads in Japan can be even weirder!

In this quiz, I'll give you a Japanese word, and you try to guess the weird trend that word refers to!

意外な傾向
UNEXPECTED TRENDS

1. Your friend has decided to go out for some ひとから *hitokara* later tonight. What will she be doing?

A Practising karate in abandoned urban buildings.

B Singing karaoke on her own, in a booth that only fits one person.

C Eating a meal that contains food of every colour in the rainbow.

D An amusement park ride that spins a group of people in every direction until one of them hits a panic button.

Answer: B. ひとから hitokara is a new trend that lets people enjoy singing, without the embarrassment of being heard singing.

>>>

デビット・ベネット DAVID BENNETT

UNEXPECTED TRENDS • 意外な傾向

2. Your brother was disciplined for playing かんちょう kanchou at school. What did he do?

A Tried to hide in plain sight in a staff meeting for as long as possible.

B Snuck under the bleachers in the gymnasium and tied together the shoelaces of numerous spectators.

C Shaped his hands like a gun, snuck up on someone, and poked them in the butt while yelling *"kanchou!"*

D Dared his friends to jump over higher and higher obstacles without spilling a cup of water.

Answer: C. かんちょう kanchou means 'enema', and for unknown reasons, this has become a common schoolyard game in Japan.

3. You hear a co-worker talking about a デコトラ *dekotora* he saw recently, covered in chrome, neon, and artwork. What did he see?

A An elaborately-decorated transport truck hauling goods.

B A roadside stand selling cellphones and fashion accessories to teens.

C A young woman participating in a new "cyber-glamour" fashion trend.

D A new kind of graffiti art installation that incorporates motorized and electrical components.

Answer: A. For those with lower budgets, デコチャリ dekochari scratches the same itch.

>>>

デビット・ベネット DAVID BENNETT

UNEXPECTED TRENDS • 意外な傾向

4. Another co-worker wants to change her look with やえば *yaeba*, but everyone in the office is urging her not to. What is she considering?

A Tattooing her eyelids, so her eyes look like they're open even when they're closed.

B Capping her upper canine teeth so that they protrude unevenly.

C Shaving a strip through her hair and pulling the rest into pig-tails.

D Applying false fingernails with embedded LED lights.

Answer: B. やえば *yaeba* is a surprisingly expensive trend among young women that creates a "snaggle-tooth" or "picket fence" look.

5. Your friend invites you out for some はちのこ *hachinoko* and beer. What will you be eating?

A Small chips of spiced cardboard, which contain no calories and pass harmlessly through the body.

B An American breakfast with eggs and unlimited hash browns. In Japan this is served with beer at dinner time.

C Special ice chips that each contain a drop of gasoline, allowing patrons to swallow them and belch flame.

D Crunchy, deep-fried bee larvae, seasoned with soy sauce and sugar.

Answer: D. They're high in protein! The beer is included to lower your natural inhibitions around EATING BEES.

WRITING RIGHT

Wherein we examine the quirks of written Japanese, from calligraphy to computer screen and in between.

Persimmon Chips? 186
For That Pen You Hate 188
Backwards Again? 194
A Tour Of The Noun Factory 196
Moon Pruner 193
Marks Of Distinction 200
It's Raining Kanji! 204
The Great Kanji Conundrum 208

正しい書き方

書く時は細部まで気を付けないと!

一番好きな果物は柿 186
手が痛い 188
逆じゃない? 194
名詞化 196
お月様の園芸 193
。ー・「」 200
漢字雨 204
漢字の難問 208

一番好きな果物は柿
PERSIMMON CHIPS?

When I type the character for 'wood chips', it comes out as 'persimmon' instead. Why?

Notice that these characters are very similar. You can see the difference here:

杮 柿

Back in the early days of computers, screens didn't display as much detail as today. In fact, the characters for 'wood chips' and 'persimmon' looked identical! This is where the problem began.

On modern computers, every character in every writing system, from A to 漢 to ᚳ to 🐢, has its own number under a system called *Unicode*.

When assigning the numbers for kanji characters, the *Unicode* people decided to assign the same number to 'wood chips' and 'persimmon', even though their meanings are completely different!

> What were they trying to do, save some extra numbers for Klingon?

Thankfully, 柿 *kokera* ('wood chips' or 'chopped wood') was recently added to *Unicode* as a separate character, finally correcting this mistake.

> Which just goes to show you, if you aren't willing to do a job right, you'd better be willing to do it again later. •

手が痛い
FOR THAT PEN YOU HATE

Which kanji character requires the most strokes?

Although there's no definitive answer to this question, here are some contenders:

- 鑑 *23 strokes*
  kagami, ***kan***
  ('mirror' or 'to look back')

- 鷹 *24 strokes*
  taka ('hawk')

- 鬣 *25 strokes*
  tategami ('lion's mane')

- 廳 *25 strokes*
  chou
  ('government office' or 'hall')

廳 is the traditional form of 庁. The simplified form 庁 is based on the Chinese character 厅.

29 strokes
utsu ('depression')

 30 strokes
hyou ('a horde of horses')

> This is the kanji character 馬 *uma* ('horse'), written three times.

 33 strokes
so or **arai** ('rough')

> This is the kanji character 鹿 *shika* ('deer'), written three times.

 48 strokes
tou
('appearance of a dragon in flight')

This is the most complex kanji character included in *Unicode*, a universal system

FOR THAT PEN YOU HATE • 手が痛い

for encoding written text on a computer. But we aren't done yet!

The kanji character that's claimed to have the most strokes of all is this 84-stroke beast, *taito*, also known as *daito/otodo*:

taito form

daito/otodo form

Taito/daito/otodo is made by combining these two characters:

 tai 'cloudy'

 tou 'appearance of a dragon in flight'

The character for 'cloudy' is itself made from three repetitions of 雲, the 12-stroke character for 'cloud'.

And, as you already know, 'appearance of a dragon in flight' is made from three repetitions of 龍, the 16-stroke character for dragon.

Altogether, that's (3×12) + (3×16) = 84!

So what does *taito* mean? Supposedly, something like 'the sight of a dragon emerging from the clouds'.

> Yeah, this is where I have to step in. *Taito* might look majestic, but it doesn't appear in standard dictionaries, and it's disputed whether it's a real character at all, or just some long-lost joke.

FOR THAT PEN YOU HATE • 手が痛い

Awww! C'mon Bento!

Taito does appear in dictionaries of *names* from 1964, 1977, and 1990. And in 2000 it apparently was used as the name of a ramen shop in Chiba Prefecture. However, it doesn't appear in any Chinese dictionaries at all.

So is it a legitimate made-in-Japan kanji character, or a hoax that became a real word? Nobody knows for sure. •

お月様の園芸
MOON PRUNER

Why is 'the man in the moon' written with the characters 桂男 *katsuraotoko*, meaning 'aromatic tree man'?

This name comes from a Chinese legend.

In the story, there's a man who lives in a great palace on the moon. He spends his time pruning and chopping away at a gigantic Katsura tree which grows there.

As he prunes the tree, the shape of the moon shrinks and becomes a crescent, until there's almost nothing left. The tree then slowly grows its branches back. This accounts for the waxing and waning of the moon. •

逆じゃない?
BACKWARDS AGAIN?

I picked up a manga to browse it today and the ending of the story was on the first page. Total spoiler! Why did they do that?

Because Japanese books are traditionally read from right to left.

Japanese text is traditionally written in vertical columns, and you read those columns starting at the right side of the page and continuing toward the left.

So, it's only logical that the front cover of a book would be at the right side, and the back cover at the left side.

This is the opposite of English, which is written in horizontal rows. You read those rows from left to right, starting at the top of the page and moving downward.

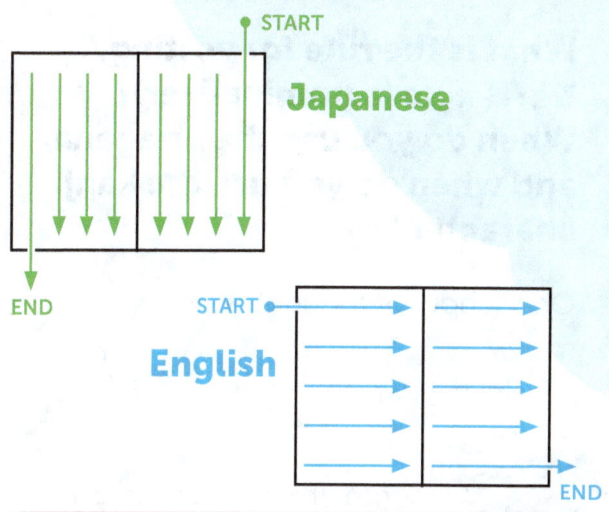

Nowadays, Japanese books can be found in both left-to-right and right-to-left formats.

The text on each page can also be found in either traditional Japanese style (top-to-bottom, right-to-left) or English style (top-to-bottom, left-to-right). •

名詞化
A TOUR OF THE NOUN FACTORY

What is the rule for writing こと・事 *koto* (a nominalizer)? When do you use the hiragana, and when do you use the kanji character?

One school of thought—

> Hold on, what's a nominalizer?

> I've got this. A nominalizer is something that helps you talk about a verb as if it were a noun.

> In English, you sometimes use the sound *"ation"* as a nominalizer. For example, if a local government was planning to urbanize an area, you could call that "planned urbaniz*ation*".

 In Japanese, you use *koto* to do something similar.

One school of thought suggests that the hiragana form こと should be used for uncountable things and short phrases. Meanwhile, the kanji form 事 should be used for countable things.

For example:

彼の言ってること間違ってるでしょう?
Kare no itteru koto machigatteru deshou?
What he's saying is wrong, isn't it?

Here こと *koto* is used to turn the idea "what he's saying" into a noun, so that a question can be asked about it.

A TOUR OF THE NOUN FACTORY • 名詞化

Here's another example:

主人から電話があり、
   金曜日に自宅することになった

Shujin kara denwa ga ari,
   kinyoubi ni jitaku suru koto ni natta.

(My) husband called and
   will be coming home on friday.

Here こと *koto* is used to turn the idea "coming home" into a noun, so that the speaker can say when it will happen.

> In English, both of these example sentences can be constructed without using a nominalizer.

> However, the phrase "what he's saying" still takes the role of a noun in the English sentence.

Now here's an example using the kanji form of *koto*:

昨日のセミナーでは多くの事を学んだ

Kinou no seminaa deha ooku no koto wo mananda.

In yesterday's class, I learned many things.

Here, 事 *koto* is used to turn the idea of "many" into a noun, so that it can be the object of the verb "to learn".

Because "many things" are something you could *potentially* count, the kanji form is used instead of the hiragana. •

｡ー・「」
MARKS OF DISTINCTION

Why aren't there any spaces between Japanese words? And what the heck are these guys: 『』? I thought Tetris was from Russia!

Punctuation works a little differently in Japanese. For example, spaces aren't used between words unless it's necessary to clarify the meaning. (Usually, context is enough to group characters into words.)

Here are some symbols you might encounter, along with their meaning:

- 「」 The 鈎括弧 *kagikakko* ('key brackets') are used for quoted speech.

- 『』 The 二重鈎括弧 *nijuukagikakko* ('double brackets') aren't Tetris

blocks! They're used for quotes-within-quotes, as well as for book titles, since Japanese text doesn't use *italic* type. They're sometimes also used to indicate words heard through a telephone or another device. These symbols are also known as 白括弧 *shirokakko* ('white brackets').

- ｡ The 句点 *kuten* ('period') is used to separate sentences, just like in English. However, it isn't required at the end of a sentence that stands alone, or if the sentence ends with any other punctuation.

- ､ The 読点 *touten* ('reading point') is used fairly liberally to indicate a pause or break in a sentence. It is placed at the bottom-right of the character, and no extra space is added afterward.

- **?** The 疑問符 *gimonfu* ('question mark') is not required in Japanese. Questions can simply end with a full stop, since the sentence will already contain the interrogative marker か *ka*.* However, question marks have become common in informal writing.

- **!** The 感嘆符 *kantanfu* ('exclamation mark') is also not part of formal Japanese writing, but is often used like it is in English.

- **·** The 中黒 *nakaguro* ('middle black') is used to clarify separations between words that would

---

* For more on this, see "Who Asked You?" on page 228.

otherwise form a compound. It's also used to mark lists, and to separate foreign first names from last names. For example, デビット・ベネット (David Bennett).

- 〜 The 波ダッシュ *nami dasshu* ('wave dash') is used to indicate a range of values, for example, 月〜金曜日 'Monday to Friday'. It's also used to indicate a subtitle, or for a drawn-out vowel sound.

Punctuation wasn't really used in Japanese until the 19th century, when many European texts were translated into Japanese. This explains why some marks that are crucial in other languages, like the question mark, are optional in Japanese. •

漢字雨
IT'S RAINING KANJI!

I see a lot of kanji characters with 雨 *ame* ('rain') in them. They all seem to be related to the weather, but they don't all mean 'rain'. What's going on?

Originally, 雨 *ame* was a pictogram* of a cloud with raindrops falling from it.

Nobody knows exactly how this pictogram developed into its many current uses, but the characters formed with 雨 *ame* mostly refer to things in the sky, or things formed from water or moisture.

The characters combining with 雨 may be chosen for their meanings or sounds.

* A pictogram is a written symbol that looks like a picture of the idea it represents.

Some examples involving meanings:

- 雲 *kumo* 'cloud'
  云 is a pictogram of a cloud
- 雹 *hyou* 'hail'
  包 means 'package' or 'wrapped thing'

Some examples involving sounds:

- 雷 *kaminari* 'thunder'
  田 means 'rice paddy'
- 霜 *shimo* 'frost'
  相 means 'visualize' or 'meeting'
- 雪 *yuki* 'snow'
  ヨ is a pictogram of a hand
- 霧 *kiri* 'fog'
  務 means 'be devoted' or 'pursue'
- 靄 *moya* 'mist/haze'
  謁 means 'visit' or 'pay respects'

IT'S RAINING KANJI • 漢字雨

On the other hand, when you see 雨 *ame* used as a complete character in a compound word, then that word usually does refer to rain:

大雨	*ooame*	'heavy rain'
小雨	*kosame*	'light rain'
梅雨	*tsuyu*	'rainy season'
豪雨	*gouu**	'very heavy rain'

And of course, it's also possible to talk about 'rain' without using 雨 *ame* at all, for example, 夕立 *yuudachi* ('sudden afternoon rain shower'). •

* Nowadays, many people say *goame* instead.

IT'S QUIZ TIME!

Contestants, get ready! Kanji characters are challenging to begin with. Some of them take it to the next level by looking nearly identical to one another!

On the next page, can you match each kanji character with its correct meaning?

漢字の難問
THE GREAT KANJI CONUNDRUM

1   犬   太   大

big   dog   thick

---

2   本   末   木   来   未

tree   book   end   not yet   come

---

3   天   夫

heaven   husband

---

4   官   宮

shinto shrine   government official

---

5   師   帥

teacher / mentor   military commander

気になる日本語   FLYING RABBITS AND BLUE TRAFFIC LIGHTS

Match the kanji characters up to their correct meanings!

Answers:

1.
大 **dai** ('big')   犬 **inu** ('dog')   太 **futo-(i)** ('thick')

2.
木 **ki** ('tree')   本 **hon** ('book')   末 **sue** ('end')   未 **ima-(da)** ('not yet')   来 **ku-(ru)** ('come')

3.
天 **ten** ('heaven')
夫 **otto** ('husband')

4.
吏 **tsukasa** ('government official')
宮 **omiya** ('Shinto shrine')

5.
師 **shi** ('teacher/mentor')
帥 **sotsu** ('military commander')

DAVID'S DICTION ACADEMY

Wherein David shows you just how many different ways there are to say something in Japanese . . . including the right way.

Mind Your Language 212
Counting Your Manga. 216
What Did He Just Say? 220
Just Say When 224
A Verbal Objection 226
Who Asked You? 228
Small Words, Big Trouble 230
On the Road. 235

デビットの日本語アカデミー
正しい表現を身につけよう！

言葉に気を付けて 212
漫画がありすぎる時 216
なんつって? 220
いつか知ってる? 224
文型 226
だから何? 228
言葉の助っ人 230
オン・ザ・ロード 235

言葉に気を付けて
MIND YOUR LANGUAGE

I've been trying to pick up more Japanese by listening to my friend from Japan. But I feel like she says things differently depending on who she's speaking to. What's going on?

Japanese culture has a complex sense of formality and respect, and the language reflects this. There are rules about how to speak to your boss, your employee, a customer, your elders or juniors, the opposite sex, and various other rules.

> English has this concept too, but it isn't emphasized as strongly. Choosing the right words matters, but so does body language and tone of voice . . .

> In Japanese, phrasing, grammar and vocabulary can change dramatically depending on who a person is speaking to, and the difference in social status between the listener and the speaker.

> The difference is so noticeable that a listener can easily gauge the relationship between two people by listening to how they speak to each other.

In Japanese, you can show respect with 尊敬語 *sonkeigo* ('respectful language'), 謙譲語 *kenjougo* ('humble language'), and 丁寧語 *teineigo* ('polite language').

>>>

MIND YOUR LANGUAGE • 言葉に気を付けて

尊敬語 *sonkeigo* ('respectful language') is used when the person being spoken about is of a higher rank than the speaker themselves. For example:

> 田中さんにお会いになりましたか？
> *Tanaka-san ni oaininarimashita ka?*
> Did you meet Mr. Tanaka?

謙譲語 *kenjougo* ('humble language') is used when speaking about oneself to someone of a higher rank. For example:

> 田中さんにお目にかかりました
> *Tanaka-san ni omenikakarimashita.*
> I saw Mr. Tanaka.

丁寧語 *teineigo* ('polite language') is used to show politeness or formality without specifically showing deference. It's often used in formal situations, or when ranks are similar, or when rank is unknown. For example:

> 田中さんに会いましたか？
> *Tanaka-san ni aimashita ka?*
> Did you meet Mr. Tanaka?

And finally, for contrast, here's the same question using informal speech:

> 田中さんに会った？
> *Tanaka-san ni atta?*
> Did you meet Mr. Tanaka?

Notice that the more formal and respectful the tone, the longer the utterances.

Mastering tone is essential to communicating in Japanese. It's not just what you say, but how! •

漫画がありすぎる時
COUNTING YOUR MANGA

How can I count really, really high in Japanese?

Here are the Japanese words for some extremely large numbers:

 万　まん man
10 000

 億　おく oku
100 000 000
(one hundred million)

 兆　ちょう chou
1 000 000 000 000
(one trillion)

 京　けい kei
10 000 000 000 000 000
(ten quadrillion)

 垓　がい gai
100 000 000 000 000 000 000
(one hundred quintillion)

| 秭 | じょ *jo* |

10^{24} *(one septillion)*

| 穣 | じょう *jou* |

10^{28} *(ten octillion)*

| 溝 | こう *kou* |

10^{32} *(one hundred nonillion)*

| 澗 | かん *kan* |

10^{36} *(one undecillion)*

| 正 | せい *sei* |

10^{40} *(ten duodecillion)*

| 載 | さい *sai* |

10^{44} *(one hundred tredecillion)*

| 極 | ごく *goku* |

10^{48} *(one quindecillion)*

> Now, don't forget, in English the digits are grouped by thousands (with three digits per group) . . .

>>>

デビット・ベネット DAVID BENNETT

COUNTING YOUR MANGA • 漫画がありすぎる時

So, for example, you count:

      1 000 one thousand
    10 000 ten thousand
  100 000 one hundred thousand

. . . all using the word 'thousand', and then you continue with:

    1 000 000 one million
  10 000 000 ten million
100 000 000 one hundred million

. . . all using the word 'million'.

But in Japanese, digits are grouped by ten-thousand instead (four digits per group) . . .

So, for example, you'd count:

一万　*ichi man*
'one ten-thousand'

十万　*jyuu man*
'ten ten-thousands'

百万　*hyaku man*
'one hundred ten-thousands'

一千万　*issen man*
'one thousand ten-thousands'

All of these are based on the unit 万 *man* ('ten-thousands').

You'd then proceed with the unit 億 *oku* ('hundred-millions'), and so on through the table on the previous pages. •

なんつって？
WHAT DID HE JUST SAY?

I feel like I understand Japanese fairly well, but when I hear people from the Kansai region* speak, I don't get them at all! What's wrong with me?

They're speaking 関西弁 *kansaiben*, one of many regional dialects in Japan.

Just like with English, where you live in Japan influences the way you speak. This affects intonation, pitch, vocabulary, and even the meaning of certain words.

Regional dialects are unintelligible to one another, so a native speaker from Aomori prefecture would have a very difficult time understanding anything when

---

* The Kansai region includes Osaka, Kobe, and Kyoto (*Oosaka*, *Koube*, and *Kyouto*).

speaking to someone from the island of Tanegashima.

Standard Japanese, or 標準語 *hyoujungo*, has been taught to all Japanese school children since the end of World War II in 1945. Later, in the 1970's and 1980's, there was a movement to eliminate regional dialects.

> 関西弁 *kansaiben* is one of the most famous regional dialects of Japanese.

> 大阪弁 *oosakaben*, a sub-dialect of *kansaiben*, is considered the language of commerce because of its roots in the merchant town of Osaka . . .

WHAT DID HE JUST SAY? • なんつって?

> 関西弁 *kansaiben* is also the dialect of comedy. Many famous comedians come from the Kansai region, and it's common to hear *kansaiben* on Japanese TV.

Here's an example. If you were speaking standard Japanese, and you were refusing to go somewhere, you might say:

> 行かない! *Ikanai!* I won't go!

But in 関西弁 *kansaiben*, it sounds like this:

> 行かへん! *Ikahen!* I won't go!

The negative suffix ない *nai* is replaced by へん *hen*, but the meaning of the phrase is the same. In fact, in **kansaiben** the phrase can be (and often is) shortened to just 行かん *ikan*.

Sometimes the meaning of a word can be different, even though the sound is the same. For example, in standard Japanese, まけた *maketa* means 'I lost'.

But in 讃岐弁 *sanukiben*, the regional dialect of Kagawa prefecture, 負けた *maketa* means 'I knocked it over'.

It's become less common to hear regional dialects being used in the workplace, and people have been known to suppress their dialect when working for a big firm in Tokyo. But they will quickly re-appear at family gatherings, or during New Year's and Obon! •

いつか知ってる?
JUST SAY WHEN

Is there a word for "the day before yesterday" in Japanese?

What, you'd be satisfied with just that? There are all kinds of words for different days! Here are some examples:

一昨昨日 *sakiototoi*
Three days ago

一昨日 *ototoi* or *ototsui*
The day before yesterday

昨日 *kinou*
Yesterday

今日 *kyou*
Today

明日 *asu* or *ashita*
Tomorrow

明後日 _asatte_

The day after tomorrow

明明後日 _shiasatte_

Three days from now

弥の明後日 _yanoasatte_

Four days from now

十六夜 _izayoi_

The night following the night of the full moon.

> The kanji for *izayoi* literally mean 'sixteenth night', referring to the sixteenth night that the moon has appeared in the night sky. This is the first night of the waning moon, and has a connotation of slowing, wavering, or hesitation. •

文型
A VERBAL OBJECTION

When I translate directly from Japanese, it sounds like Yoda talking. Why are some of the words in the wrong order?

In English, we order our sentences with the subject first, then the verb, then the object. For example:

I am slowly eating an apple.
SUBJECT VERB ADVERB OBJECT

In Japanese, the verb comes at the end of the sentence instead. For example:

ゆっくりリンゴを食べている
Yukkuri ringo wo tabeteiru.

This translates literally to:

slowly + apple + eating

Don't forget, in Japanese the subject of a sentence can often be assumed. So, in the sentence above (*slowly+apple+eating*), it's 'I' who is eating the apple, but the 'I' is implied.

English is called an SVO language (subject-verb-object), and Japanese is called an SOV language (subject-object-verb).

Other orders of subject, verb, and object exist around the world, but the only other common word order is VSO (about 1 in 10 languages). •

だから何？
WHO ASKED YOU?

Why do questions in Japanese not always use the Japanese words for who, what, why, when, and how?*

Because most of the time, those words aren't necessary.

> First you have to understand why we use these words in English. They help to mark the sentence as a question. (This is called an 'interrogative marker'.)

> But in Japanese, questions are already marked by putting か *ka* at the end of the sentence.

* Namely: だれ *dare* 'who', なに *nani* 'what', なぜ *naze* 'why', いつ *itsu* 'when', どう *dou* 'how'.

For example:

> お元気ですか *Ogenki* **desu** *ka?*

This phrase translates literally to . . .

> being well + [question marker]

. . . which means, "How are you doing?"

> In spoken English, you raise your tone at the end of a sentence to reinforce that it's a question. In writing, you use a question mark for the same purpose.

> In Japanese, you also raise your tone when speaking, but the question mark isn't necessary in writing. However, its use is becoming more common. •

言葉の助っ人
SMALL WORDS, BIG TROUBLE

I keep making mistakes when I try to translate simple words like 'from', 'to', and 'also'. Why are the simple words so hard?

You've discovered particles!

> I had that happen with my soup the other day.

In English, we use prepositions (like in, on, about, before) and conjunctions (like and, or, because) to help us connect different parts of sentences.

In Japanese, there's a similar (but much more complex) system, involving more than a hundred 'particles' and other grammatical markers that have various purposes:

- marking the subject and object of a sentence (が *ga*, を *wo*);

- marking the topic or indicating a contrast (は *wa*);

- showing a contrast or comparison between two things (より *yori*);

- constructing complete and incomplete lists of items (や *ya*, し *shi*);

- acting the way a preposition or conjunction would in English (と *to*, に *ni*, へ *he*, で *de*);

. . . and many others.

> Like everything else in Japanese, the system of particles is influenced by status and social situation . . .

>>>

SMALL WORDS, BIG TROUBLE • 言葉の助っ人

. . . For example, the particle だ *da*, which loosely translates to 'is', can sometimes be replaced by です *desu* to increase the politeness of the statement.

俺の友達だ！ *Ore no tomodachi da!*
This *is* my friend!
(As said to your other friends.)

僕の友達です *Boku no tomodachi desu.*
This *is* my friend.
(As said to your friend's parents.)

Actually, だ *da* and です *desu* are technically copulas (a word that links the subject of a sentence to information about the subject), but your point stands.

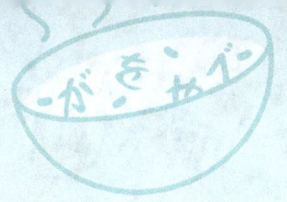

Here are some other common particles:

で de *(similar to 'in' or 'at')*
日本語で手紙を書きます
Nihongo de tegami wo kakimasu.
I will write a letter in Japanese.

へ e *(similar to 'towards' or 'to')*
日本へようこそ！
Nihon e youkoso!
Welcome to Japan!

は wa *(can be used to show contrast)*
犬は好きです
Inu wa suki desu.
I like dogs [as opposed to, say, cats].

Personally, I find fish much more calming . . .

IT'S QUIZ TIME!

Contestants, get ready! After a hard day of learning at David's Diction Academy, what could be more fun than a road trip?

See if you can guess the meaning of these *waseieigo** words. Here's a hint: they're all related to cars or driving!

* See "At the Viking Buffet" on page 79 for a full explanation of *waseieigo*!

オン・ザ・ロード
ON THE ROAD

Guess the meaning of these words:

1. ハンドル *handoru*
2. サイドブレーキ *saido bureeki*
3. フロントガラス *furonto garasu*
4. オープンカー *oopun kaa*
5. バックミラー *bakku miraa*
6. パンク *panku*
7. エンスト *ensuto*

Answers:
1. steering wheel ("handle")
2. parking brake ("side break")
3. windshield ("front glass")
4. convertible ("open car")
5. rearview mirror ("back mirror")
6. flat tire ("puncture")
7. stall ("engine stop")

デビット・ベネット DAVID BENNETT

ひらがな50音表
TABLE OF HIRAGANA

	a	i	u	e	o
	あ	い	う	え	お
k	か	き	く	け	こ
s	さ	し	す	せ	そ
t	た	ち	つ	て	と
n	な	に	ぬ	ね	の
h	は	ひ	ふ	へ	ほ
m	ま	み	む	め	も
y	や		ゆ		よ
r	ら	り	る	れ	ろ
w	わ	ゐ*		ゑ*	を

ん (n without vowel)

obsolete or near-obsolete

David wanted to go easy on you, so we laid these charts out the English way: left-to-right and top-to-bottom . . .

カタカナ50音表
TABLE OF KATAKANA

	a	i	u	e	o
	ア	イ	ウ	エ	オ
k	カ	キ	ク	ケ	コ
s	サ	シ	ス	セ	ソ
t	タ	チ	ツ	テ	ト
n	ナ	ニ	ヌ	ネ	ノ
h	ハ	ヒ	フ	ヘ	ホ
m	マ	ミ	ム	メ	モ
y	ヤ		ユ		ヨ
r	ラ	リ	ル	レ	ロ
w	ワ	ヰ*		ヱ*	ヲ

ン (n without vowel)

obsolete or near-obsolete

. . . in Japanese, you'd see them written vertically, from right-to-left!

デビット・ベネット DAVID BENNETT

FULL LIST OF ENTRIES

A

ABC Sutra 72
A Humble Greeting 38
All My Friend. 94
...And Sometimes A Little 156
A Precise Beard 119
A Precise River 110
Asking Precisely 112
A Tour Of The Noun Factory 196
At the Viking Buffet 79
A Verbal Objection 226

B

Backwards Again? 194
Ballad Of The Ticket-Counter 60
Become One With Broccoli. 53
Being Contradictory 107
Blue Means Go. 90
Both Fists Bump? 134
Brown Means Tea 96
Bye, I'm Home! 36

C-E

Counting The Ways To Count 50
Counting Underpants 56

Counting Your Manga.................. 216
Crimson Means Red 99
DIY Kanji 70
Extreme Counting Showdown 65

F-H
Flying Rabbits?...................... 54
For That Pen You Hate 188
From Russia With Salt 78
Harbouring Differences 120
Holy Mackerel! I've Been Robbed! 24

I
I Hate Not Losing!.................... 98
Is Ten Minutes Enough? 172
It's Pronounced "Confusing" 136
It's Raining Kanji!.................... 204
It's Windy Up Here! 150

J-L
Jumping Birds?....................... 135
Just Say When 224
Kanji in a Box 144
Konnichi What? 76
Lost In Translation 86

FULL LIST OF ENTRIES

M-N

Marks Of Distinction	200
Meaty Sarcasm	32
Mind Your Language	212
Moon Pruner	193
Not All Sushi Is Created Equal	58

O-R

On the Road	235
Persimmon Chips?	186
Precisely Lying Down	114
Precisely Vague	127
Proverbial Japanese	41
Respecting Mr. Fuji	163
Ring, Baby, Ring!	170

S

Sai vs. Sai	124
Small Words, Big Trouble	230
Sometimes It Takes A Lot…	153
Spittin' Samurai	26
Stretched Octopus??	22
Sunday Again??	140

T

- Thank You Is Difficult 173
- The Disappearance of Wi 168
- The Evolution Of Wa 102
- The Great Kanji Conundrum 208
- The Roots of Wasabi 176
- Third Floor Two Ways? 62
- This Is A Hard One 116
- Too Close to Home 164
- Trouble At Midnight 162

U-Z

- Unexpected Trends 179
- What About Dancing Shrimp? 122
- What Did He Just Say? 220
- Which Country?? 159
- Who Asked You? 228
- Worse Than Two-Faced 166
- You Need To Go The Whole 19.64km 30

項目一覧

。─・「」	200
19.64キロまで	30
ABCスートラ	72
いつか知ってる?	224
オン・ザ・ロード	235
お月様の園芸	193
お茶はブラウン	96
きく?きく。	112
ことわざ	41
この文字って何?	168
これはハード	116
こんにち何?	76
サバの泥棒	24
さようなら、帰って来たよ!	36
サンキューは難しい	173
だから何?	228
なんつって?	220
バイキングのバイキング	79
パンツを数える	56
フィストバンプ?	134
ブロッコリーの一つ…	53
ロシアより塩を込めて	78

ロスト・イン・トランスレーション	86
「わ」の進化	102
ワサビの根	176
一番好きな果物は柿	186
丁寧な挨拶	38
三階はなんで特別なの？	62
侍のカウボーイ	26
十分足りる？	172
友達はひとりじゃない！	94
同じ漢字、違う発音	136
名詞化	196
夜の問題	162
天気予報	120
寿司は色々	58
少年よ、「曖昧」を抱け	127
「山」は「やま」の時もある	163
引っ張られてるタコ？	22
意外と複雑	60
意外と言いにくい	153
意外と言いやすい	156
意外な傾向	179
手が痛い	188

デビット・ベネット DAVID BENNETT

項目一覧

数えてみよう!	65
数え方を数えよう!	50
文型	226
「日」ってすごい	140
本当に赤でしょう?	99
歳・才	124
漢字の難問	208
漢字圏の国	159
漢字雨	204
漫画がありすぎる時	216
矛か盾。どっち?!	107
(細) ヒゲ	119
(細) 川	110
(細) 横になる	114
細かすぎ	164
肉のある皮肉	32
自作漢字	70
裏表があるよりも	166
言葉に気を付けて	212
言葉の助っ人	230
説文解字	144
負けたい!	98

踊っているエビって何？	122
逆じゃない？	194
青で進め！	90
風が強い！	150
飛べるウサギ？	54
鳥のジャンプ？	135
鳴らせ！	170

デビット・ベネット DAVID BENNETT　245

INDEX

Page numbers indicate the start of the relevant entry or quiz.

1946 spelling reforms	102, 168
ame (雨)	204
aoshingou (青信号)	90
arigatou (有り難う)	173
aromatic tree man	193
Asuka period *(538–710, Japan)*	173
ateji (当て字)	176
ban (番)	65
Bento	
being teased	56, 79, 99, 102, 107, 114
teasing blossom	32, 166
Buddhism	32, 41, 54, 72, 159
cat's face, putting on the	41
chairo (茶色)	96
charinko (チャリンコ)	170
China	
history	
Ming dynasty *(1368–1644)*	136
Song dynasty *(960–1279)*	136
Southern and Northern dynasties	136
Tang dynasty *(618–907)*	136
legends	193

Chinese
    characters 14, 72, 136, 144, 150, 188, 193
chokkagatajishin (直下型地震) 164
chou (丁) 56, 65
christmas cake 166
colours 90, 96, 99
copula 230
counter 48, 50–65, 172
cyber-glamour 179
da (だ) 230
day before yesterday, the 224
de (で) 230
dekotora (デコトラ) 179
desu (です) 230
die without wrong-doing 72
dragon emerging from the clouds, sight of . . 188
e (へ)
    direction marker 102
    particle 230
    river 110
ebi (海老・蝦) 122
Edo period *(1603–1868, Japan)* 136, 200
even monkeys fall from trees 41
existing is difficult 173
eyelid tattoos 179

INDEX

facial hair	119
fujisan (富士山)	163
Genji Monogatari	173
gimonfu (疑問符)	200
go on (呉音)	136
gorioshi (ごり押し)	30
gou (合)	65
Great Hanshin Earthquake *(1995, Japan)*	164
hachinoko (はちのこ)	179
harabai (腹這い)	114
Heian period *(794-1185, Japan)*	98, 173
hen (片)	60
hige (髭・髯・鬚)	119
hiniku (皮肉)	32
hipparidako (引っ張りだこ)	22
hiragana	14
memory aid (*iroha*)	72
retired characters	72, 168
table of hiragana	236
hitokara (ひとから)	179
homonym	112
hon (**本**)	60, 65
honourific	94, 163
horse's ear, whispering a sutra in	41
humble language (*kenjougo*)	38, 212
hyoujungo (標準語)	220

ide (山上復有山)	153
ideograph	144
ikura (いくら)	78
informal speech	76, 212
interrogative marker	200, 228
iroha	72
irony	32
izayoi (十六夜)	224
jankenpon (両拳碰)	134

Japan
    culture & traditions 162, 166, 179
    history
        Asuka period *(538–710)* 173
        Edo period *(1603–1868)* 136, 200
        Great Hanshin Earthquake *(1995)* 164
        Heian period *(794-1185)* 98, 173
        Joumon period *(14,000–300 BCE)* 102
        Kamakura period *(1185–1333)* 168
        Meiji period *(1868-1912)* 150
        Post-WW2 . . . . 102, 166, 168, 170, 220
        Taishou era *(1912–1926)* 168

Japanese
    grammar
        copula 230
        counter 48, 50–65, 172
        honourific 94, 163

INDEX

    interrogative marker............ 200, 228
    nominalizer 196
    particle............................ 230
    topic marker 102, 230
    word order 226
greetings........................ 36, 38, 76
loan words 78, 150, 156
politeness and formality............38, 76, 94, 163, 212, 230
question formation..................... 228
sayings and proverbs 20, 22–41
spoken Japanese
    dialects............................ 220
    pronunciation 13
    voicing 62
written Japanese
    punctuation........................ 200
    reading direction 194
    well-known texts 173
    writing systems.................... 14
jitensha (自転車) 170
Joumon period *(14,000–300 BCE, Japan)*... 102
jyuppun • jyuubun (十分) 172
ka (か) 228
kagikakko (鉤括弧) 200
kaii moji (会意文字)................... 144

Kamakura period *(1185–1333, Japan)*	168
kan (貫)	58
kan on (漢音)	136
kanchou (かんちょう)	179
kanji (漢字)	14, 70, 132
ateji	176
classification	144
compounds	32, 144, 153
country names	159
distinctions and correct use	22, 99, 110, 116, 119, 122, 134, 135, 150, 196, 204
five or more syllables	156
made in japan (*kokuji* 国字)	70
meanings	173, 176, 188, 204
most strokes	188
readings	76, 136, 163
many readings	140
similar appearance	208
with many meanings	140
kansaiben (関西弁)	220
kantanfu (感嘆符)	200
kan-you-on (慣用音)	136
kasha moji (仮借文字)	144
katai (固い・堅い・硬い)	116
katakana	14
table of katakana	237

INDEX

katsuraotoko (桂男) 193
kawa (川・河) 110
keisei moji (形声文字) 144
kenjougo (謙譲語) 212
kiku (聞く・聴く・訊く) 112
kiru (きる) 127
kokera (柿) 186
kokuji (国字) 70
konnichi wa (今日は) 76
koto (こと・事) 196
kou
 口 (counter) 65
 紅 (crimson) 96, 99
 江 (river) 110
koucha (紅茶) 96
kouhaku utagassen (紅白歌合戦) 99
kouka (こうか) 127
koushi (こうし) 127
Kuukai (buddhist monk) 72
kuku (八十一) 153
kun-yomi (訓読み) 76, 136
kuten (句点) 200
mai (枚) 56, 60
makezugirai (負けず嫌い) 98
maki (巻) 58
makizushi 58

man in the moon	193
Manyoushuu	173
Meiji period *(1868-1912, Japan)*	150
Ming dynasty *(1368–1644, China)*	136
monkeys fall from trees	41
moshimoshi (もしもし)	38
nail that sticks out, the	41
nakaguro (中黒)	200
nami dasshu (波ダッシュ)	200
neko wo kaburu (猫を被る)	41
nigirizushi	58
nihon (日本, Japan)	140
nihongo (日本語, Japanese)	144
nijuukagikakko (二重鉤括弧)	200
niyakeru (にやける)	26
nominalizer	196
numbers	14, 62, 172
counting	50
really big numbers	216
o (を)	102
ocha (お茶)	96
on top of one mountain comes another	153
oni with an iron club	41
onomatopoeia	170
on-yomi (音読み)	76, 136
pangram	72

INDEX

particles	230
pictogram	144, 204
poking people in the butt	179
polite language (*teineigo*)	212
Post-WW2 Japan	90, 102, 168, 170, 220
prawn	122
rabbits, flying	54
ramen	188
red-and-white year-end song festival	99
respectful language (*sonkeigo*)	212
saba wo yomu (サバを読む)	26
sai (歳・才)	124
sankai (三階)	62
sara (皿)	58
sarcasm	32
sayounara (さようなら)	36
shichimenchou (七面鳥)	166
shiji moji (指事文字)	144
shirokakko (白括弧)	200
shoukei moji (象形文字)	144
sixteenth night, the	224
Song dynasty (*960–1279, China*)	136
sonkeigo (尊敬語)	212
Southern and Northern dynasties (*420–589, China*)	136
SOV word order	226

sudden afternoon rain shower	204
sumimasen (すみません)	173
sushi	58
sutra, whispering in a horse's ear	41
SVO word order	226
tadaima (ただいま)	36
taifuu (台風)	150
Taishou era *(1912–1926, Japan)*	168
taito • daito • otodo	188
tako (たこ)	22
Tang dynasty *(618–907, China)*	136
tea	96
teineigo (丁寧語)	212
tenchuu moji (転注文字)	144
tidal wave	120
tobacco	26
tobihaneru (飛び跳ねる)	54
tobu (とぶ)	135
tomodachi (友達)	94
topic marker	102, 230
touten (読点)	200
tou on (唐音)	136
traffic lights, blue	90
tsunami (津波)	120
tsundoku (積読)	*inside front cover*
underwear	56

デビット・ベネット DAVID BENNETT

INDEX

unicode	186, 188
units of measurement	30, 156
utsubuse (うつ伏せ)	114
Utsuho Monogatari	173
utsuru (うつる)	127
voicing	62

wa
- 羽 (counter for rabbits) 54
- は (particle indicating contrast) 230
- は (topic marker) 102

wasabi (山葵・わさび)	58, 176
waseieigo (和製英語)	79, 86, 235
we (ゑ, retired character)	168
whispering a sutra in a horse's ear	41
wi (ゐ, retired character)	168
wo (を, semi-retired character)	168

women
- if three gather 41

yaeba (やえば)	179
yahan (夜半)	162
yaku (やく)	127
yani sagaru (ヤニ下がる)	26
yasu (休)	144
yuujin (友人)	94
zu (ず)	98

Other Books by David Bennett

外資系社長が出合った 不思議すぎる日本語
ISBN 978-4-04-604605-5
The Japanese edition of *Flying Rabbits and Blue Traffic Lights*, done in a manga style with short essays. Available from KADOKAWA and on Amazon.jp in print and ebook format.

www.ingramcontent.com/pod-product-compliance
Lightning Source LLC
Chambersburg PA
CBHW070652120526
44590CB00013BA/922